YORK'S GOLDEN HALF MILE

THE STORY *of* CONEY STREET

Van Wilson

York Archaeological Trust, 2013

Published by York Archaeological Trust 2013
47 Aldwark, York YO1 7BX
www.yorkarchaeology.co.uk

All rights reserved

Van Wilson hereby asserts and gives notice of her right under Section 77 of the
Copyright, Designs and Patents Act 1988 to be identified as the author of this work.

No part of this publication may be reproduced, stored in a retrieval system
or transmitted in any form or by any means without prior written
permission from the publisher.

Printed by B&B Press
Rotherham

ISBN No. 978-1 874454 64 9

Front cover: *Coney Street c. 1900*
Back cover: *Leak and Thorp assistants and maids c. 1920;*
            Fire at Leak and Thorp, 1933 (Ian Collinson)
Inside covers: *Bird's eye view of Coney Street, by Ridsdale Tate, 1914*
            (Hugh Murray/Peter Stanhope)

CONTENTS

ACKNOWLEDGEMENTS

We would like to thank the following for their generous support in the funding of this publication: Friends of York Archaeological Trust, Robert Kiln Charitable Trust, Sheldon Memorial Trust, Patricia and Donald Shepherd Charitable Trust, Sylvia and Colin Shepherd Memorial Trust, Noel G. Terry Charitable Trust, York Common Good Trust, Yorkshire Architectural and York Archaeological Society and Yorkshire Philosophical Society.

I would like to thank the following who shared their stories, and photographs of Coney Street with me: Carol Addy, Dawn Allerston, John Avison, Edward Bacon, James Barker, Lady Gillian Barron, John Boardman, Suzy Brown, Val Cason, Alwyn Cammidge, Ian Collinson, June Dandy, Eileen Dickenson, Brian Douglass, Chris and John Dowell, Gill Fox, Patsie Hirstwood, Malcolm Huntington, Keith Hyman, Ernest and Moyra Johnson, Sheila Keane, Eileen Kelly, Malcolm McManahan, Joan Moat, Susan Natt, Rev Jane Nattress, Catherine Pickard, Janet and Peter Pigott, Alan Powell, Jean Rudka, Joan Sadler, Anne Sains, Joan Sargent, Michael Saville, Bill Simpson, Nina Smith, Catherine Suter, Edith Tavender, Tina Territt, Brian Wilson, David Wilson, Alma and David Winship.

For supplying photographs I would also like to thank Ann Gordon, James Grisdale, Hugh Murray, Ann Platt of the Civic Office, Derek Ralphs, Peter Stanhope and York Oral History Society; David Poole for information and Mike Race for his photographs, for copying many of the photographs and for helping with transport to interviews.

I wish to thank the Honourable Lord Mayor for 2013, Councillor Julie Gunnell, for the foreword of this book. From York Archaeological Trust I would like to thank Sarah Maltby, Director of Attractions, Mike Andrews for scanning photographs, Lesley Collett for her photo-editing, design and typesetting of the book, but in particular I am indebted to Christine Kyriacou, Editor and Archivist, for managing the project, for her successful fundraising, painstaking proofreading and ongoing support.

FOREWORD
by Councillor Julie Gunnell,
The Right Honourable The Lord Mayor of York 2013–2014

This book is a wonderful record of life in Coney Street as seen through the eyes of those who have lived or worked in the area from the 1920s onwards. Coney Street is now a modern shopping street, but it has a long and interesting history going back to Roman times. More recently it housed exclusive fashion establishments, family businesses, a press office, hotels and pubs. It was such an exclusive area at one time that it was dubbed 'York's Golden Half Mile'.

Today the Guildhall and Mansion House stand little changed at the end of Coney Street, but the rest of the street has been transformed. I have seen huge changes within my lifetime in York, with the disappearance of so many family-run and independent businesses. To have this documented in such an accessible fashion is tremendous.

As Lord Mayor at the time of publication of this book, I am very pleased to be associated with it. Both the Mansion House, my home for this year, and the adjacent Guildhall feature in the book. I have always greatly valued working within the local community, and think that this book, which sets out to record history as experienced by local people themselves, is very important.

I would like to wish the author, Van Wilson, and York Archaeological Trust every success with this book and with future oral history projects which make so great a contribution to York's social and cultural heritage.

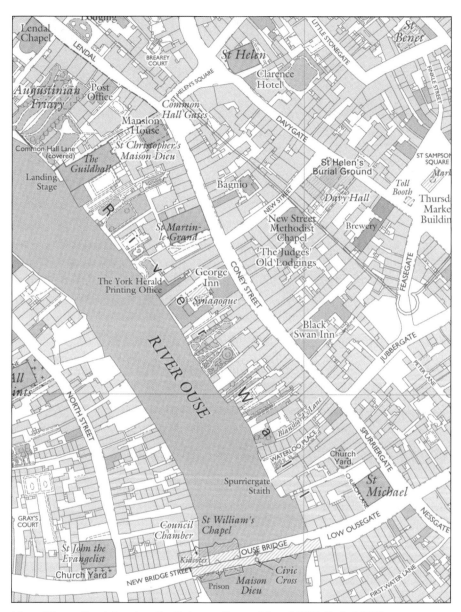

Map of Coney Street, based on the Ordnance Survey Map of 1852. Scale 1:2500

(First published in the British Historic Towns Atlas, volume V, York.

© The Historic Towns Trust and York Archaeological Trust 2013)

— Chapter 1 —
THE EARLY YEARS *of* CONEY STREET

The street now called Coney Street was originally the road parallel with the south western wall of the city's Roman fortress in the first century AD, the road between the legionary fortress and the River Ouse. A document of 1150 reveals that it was called Cuningstrete, the King's Street, and it ran from Ousegate right up to the Museum Gardens, with Old Coney Street (Auld Conynstrete) at one end (now called Lendal), and Little Coney Street at the Ousegate end. The latter became Spurriergate, the name first recorded in 1538 as the street of the spurmakers. The two churches in Coney Street, St Martin le Grand and St Michael, Spurriergate, are mentioned in the Domesday Book. Unusually, Coney Street has always been in three parishes, St Martin le Grand, St Michael, Spurriergate and St Helen, now in Davygate.

Coney Street is one of the few city centre streets to retain the Anglo-Saxon 'street' rather than the Danish 'gate'. In the 12th century, it was part of the Jewish quarter, and Aaron of York, once the wealthiest Jew in England, until royal taxation stripped him of his fortune and left him in poverty, lived next door but one to St Martin's, on the site of what became the George Inn, later Leak and Thorp and today a group of shops including Next and River Island. In the anti Jewish riots of 1190, Aaron's property was burnt down though he escaped. Aaron's father, Joceus or Josce, took his wealth and some of his family to York Castle before his home was destroyed. The Jewish people were besieged in the Castle by the mob who ordered them to deny their religion. The Jews offered money for their freedom but were refused. Many then took their own lives, others died in the flames, and the rest, who surrendered, were massacred. C B Knight in his history of York called the tragedy, 'The worst and most deplorable outrage ever perpetrated within the city of York'. A plaque to commemorate this dreadful day stands at Clifford's Tower.

In medieval times, four of the stations of the Corpus Christi wagon plays were in Coney Street. There were three common lanes leading down from the street to the Ouse. Common Hall Lane (sometimes called Stonegate Landing) was opposite the entrance of Stonegate (before St Helen's Square existed) and is now underneath the present Guildhall. St Martin's Lane, first mentioned in the 1160s, was called Kyrklane in 1390, and Old Lane by 1702, and ran down beside St Martin's Church. The third lane, Blanchard's Lane (named after the one time proprietor of the York Chronicle) ran along the parish boundary, on the cusp of Coney Street and Spurriergate, opposite what is now Market Street. The lanes were used for the shipping and landing of goods, including coal. In the 12th and 13th centuries, the imposing mansion Davy Hall sat on what is now New Street and part of Davygate. It was the home of the Le Lardiner family, who were custodians of the Forest of Galtres.

In 1308 Coney Street was described as York's principal street for business, but it was not for another century and a half that it became much more significant. In 1459 the Guildhall, designed by Robert Couper, was built, near to the Gild of St Christopher Maison Dieu (almshouse), which was founded in York in 1396. The Gild Hall as it was originally called, was designed as a meeting place to celebrate the feasts of the York Gilds. It was also used as a theatre for performances in the 16th century by itinerant companies of actors.

The opening of the George Inn in 1614 also gave more prominence to the street, as a coaching hostelry for mail and passenger coaches, with travellers lodging there before undertaking the four day journey to London. (The journey was cut to 20 hours by 1836). The landlord Thomas Kaye had been Sheriff of York in 1614, and he bought the premises, previously called the Bull then the Rose, rebuilt and renamed it. The Rockingham Masonic Lodge held its meetings in the Inn. Many well-known people stayed there over the years, including the Water Poet, John Taylor, in 1622, architect and dramatist John Vanbrugh, (who was married in York in 1719), the poet Shelley and the Brontë sisters. Another coaching inn, the Black Swan, which was further down the street on the site of the present British Home Stores, was first mentioned in 1663, and once stabled 130 horses.

The 18th-century Mansion House (David Wilson)

The greatest changes in Coney Street were in the 18th and early 19th centuries, by which time it was called Conyng Street (as shown on a map of 1736). The Mansion House of course was built in 1725–32 on the site of St Christopher's Chapel, 14 years before its London counterpart. After the Dissolution in 1547, St Christopher's Chapel was converted into a house, and demolished in 1725. The Merchant Adventurers met in the Guildhall and the Mansion House until 1815. The area in front of the Mansion House was paved in 1777, and in 1782 the houses facing the building were pulled down to form the open square which exists today.

In 1734 on the corner of Spurriergate was the bank of Raper, Swann and Co, the oldest bank in the city. By 1810 there were three banks in the city, and this one had moved to the corner of New Street. It was taken over by Beckett & Co in 1879. In 1735 Alexander Staples, from London, moved the York Courant newspaper offices into a house in Coney Street opposite St Martin's Church. Once Staples retired, it was owned by Ward and Chandler, booksellers. The Bagnio, which was behind it, became a printing office in 1738. This Turkish bath had been erected in 1691 in the alley leading off Coney Street to the Leopard Inn.

John Wesley visited the area when he preached in St Michael's in the 1770s and 1780s. There was also a private school in Spurriergate, set up in 1776 by George Brown. The Yorkshire Fire and Life Insurance Company began life in 1824 and had its first offices in Coney Street, before it moved to St Helen's Square, and later Rougier Street. It has gone through many guises to eventually become Aviva. William Etty, the York painter, who helped to save the bar walls and Bootham Bar from demolition, returned to York from his travels in 1846, buying a house and studio in Coney Street overlooking the river. When he died in 1849, there was a huge turn out for the funeral.

In both 1769 and 1841, Coney Street was widened for coaches going to the Black Swan and the George, and to balls in the Assembly Rooms

Bagnio – the Turkish bath (David Wilson)

in Blake Street. Building in the street had been carried out at various times, hence the variety of architecture. Examples from the 16th century include the house at number 32, with a brick-lined 15th century well in its yard and the three-storey timber-framed building at the corner of New Street, for many years the House of Bewlay tobacconist, but now a mobile phone shop. The House of Bewlay was founded by Edward Allen, father of the Royal Shakespeare Company actor Patrick Allen, who had been a tobacco farmer in Malawi. The York shop was renowned for its pipes and good quality tobacco but closed in the 1990s. The house at number 16, occupied by Henry Sotheran the bookseller in 1761, still retains some Georgian fittings, though it was renovated in 1927 and 1960. The firm still exists in London where Henry moved it in 1815, and claims to be the longest established antiquarian bookseller in the world, known for acquiring the libraries of Dickens and Laurence Sterne. Behind numbers 28 and 30 is the Judges' Court, containing an early 18th century house, used as the Judges' Lodging until 1806 when it moved to Lendal. It has two storeys, attics and basement with a large courtyard both in front and behind it.

In 1900 Sotheran's shop on the corner of New Street had become Arthur Anderson, bookseller, stationer and printer, related to Anderson's tailor's. It was renovated in 1927 when plaster rendering was removed and period style windows inserted on the the ground floor, replaced by plate glass in 1960.

Coney Street 1911 (York Illustrated 1911)

In the 19th century the street was home to many small shops including linen and woollen drapers, pianoforte warehouses, grocers, picture dealers, chemists, watchmakers and jewellers, tobacconists, stationers, milliners, shoe makers, and many of these had their own warehouses in the rear of the store. There were also a number of offices for solicitors, architects, house agents, stockbrokers and two registries for servants.

Coney Street decorated for the Coronation of King George VI, 1937 (Ian Collinson)

Today the Guildhall and Mansion House still stand majestically at the end of Coney Street, but the rest of the street is vastly different from previous centuries. It could be almost any high street in Britain, or even Europe, with national and international shops, such as River Island (stores in Europe and franchises in the Middle East), TK Maxx (240 stores in Britain and Ireland) and Starbuck's, which has branches everywhere from Shanghai to Delhi, New York to Los Angeles. The small individual shops are now replaced by mobile phone stores and Poundland.

The exclusive fashion houses, family businesses and personal service may be long gone, but there are still those who remember those times with affection. Some of their stories are featured in this book.

Bird's eye view of Coney Street,
by Ridsdale Tate, 1914

(Hugh Murray/Peter Stanhope)

Chapter 2

THE GUILDHALL *and*
THE MANSION HOUSE

Although the Mansion House and Guildhall were built two and a half centuries apart, the two have long been closely linked together and are both administered by City of York Council.

The York Memorandum Book refers to a Guildhall in Coney Street in 1378, above the common lane which ran down to the river. But the hall was too small and was replaced, as the result of an agreement between the Mayor and the Commonalty in 1446, by one designed by Robert Couper. The original pillars were from trees in the Forest of Galtres. It was largely used as a meeting place for the guilds, who controlled trade within the city, and for assemblies, feasts and important events in York. In the 16th century the hall was also used for performances by itinerant bands of actors, until the audience damaged the furnishings and doors in 1592, which called a halt to the entertainment. One of the highlights of the Victorian era was a sumptuous banquet held with Prince Albert as the guest of honour in 1850. The building was the meeting place for York Corporation (from 1891), and the Council continues to meet in the Council Chamber. The annual Freedom Court, where men and women become Freemen of York, is also held there.

King Richard III, whose remains have been discovered in Leicester, enjoyed a lavish banquet at the Guildhall, and a plaque there mentions his 'great labour, good and benevolent lordship for the honour of this City'.

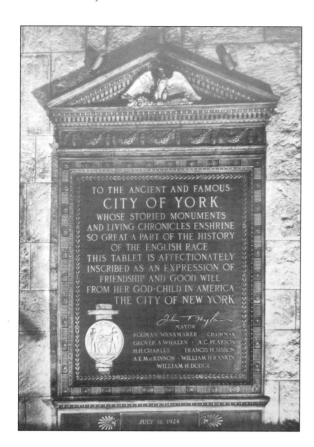

Plaque in Guildhall from New York (David Wilson)

Damage was incurred during the Civil War in the mid 17th century, but the Guildhall's darkest hour was the Baedeker raid of April 1942 when incendiary bombs fell and the inside was devastated, though the stone walls escaped. (One of the few fittings to survive was a plaque to the right of the dais, given by the city of New York in 1924). It took some years to rebuild, and the Queen Mother reopened it in 1960. It had been partly financed by the War Damage Commission. The ceremony was attended by the Oberburgermeister and Oberstadtsdirektor of Münster (which was twinned with York after the Second World War, when the city became a major base for British forces in Germany). The town of Münster also funded the wrought iron balustrade.

As the seat of civic government in York, the Guildhall in 1905 housed the Town Clerk's Office, City Engineer and Surveyor's Office, Building Inspector's Office, City Accountant's Office, Inspector of Nuisances Office, Medical Officer's Office, Ouse Navigation Trustees and Foss Navigation Office and the Court of Record. Most of these later disappeared or moved to St Leonard's Place. With the move of the City of York Council offices to Station Rise, there is now debate about the future use of the Guildhall.

Excavation at Guildhall by York Archaeological Trust, 2012.
L to R: Lord Mayor Keith Hyman, Councillor Sonja Crisp, Professor Mick Aston
(York Archaeological Trust)

In 2012, as part of the York 800 celebrations, (800 years since York got its Royal charter), York Archaeological Trust was commissioned to conduct the very first dig in the grounds of the Guildhall. Three trenches were dug, one in the Guildhall itself, one beneath the arch of the Mansion House and one in Common Lane beneath the Guild-hall. (Common Lane leads down to the river, and through a locked gate onto the riverside. At this point goods were brought into the city, including the stone used to build the Minster). Various items were found, including a comb from the Viking era, fragments of Roman pottery, a wig-curler from the early 18th century, and part of the wall of the original Common Hall.

The Lord Mayor is the first citizen of York. Although there have been Lord Mayors in York since 1217, they initially spent their year of office

Lord Mayor Rhodes Brown with Blue Coat School boys outside Guildhall 1932. Jock Wilson with mace, and Arthur Wright precede the Mayor (David Wilson)

Yorkshire mace bearers and sword bearers outside Guildhall 1935. Jock Wilson seated third from left with sword, Bill Simpson next to him with mace. (David Wilson)

in their own homes, which proved difficult when it came to entertaining. It became apparent that there was a need for a place to house both the Lord Mayor and the official insignia.

The foundation stone of the Mansion House was laid in 1725 though it was not completed until 1732. The Mansion House was said to be designed by Richard Boyle, Earl of Burlington, though more recent scholars have questioned this and William Etty (the architect, not the artist) is thought to have designed the frontage. It was built on the site of the Cross Keys Inn, previously the chapel of the Guild of St Christopher. Each Lord Mayor automatically becomes steward of the plate and insignia. This includes the Large Cup, 24 carat gold and worth £50,000, presented to the Lord Mayor by Marmaduke Rawdon in 1672. It is only used to toast the reigning sovereign.

It was not until 1941 that the city had its first female Lord Mayor, Edna Annie Crichton. Since then there have been eleven women (eight since the year 2000), and the new Lord Mayor in 2013 is Labour councillor, Julie Gunnell.

On ceremonial occasions, the Lord Mayor wears full robes and is preceded, by royal decree, by the mace bearer and the sword bearer. The latter traditionally wore the scarlet, ermine trimmed Cap of Maintenance. The first Cap was presented to the city by Richard II in 1393. The City Arms are embroidered on it. The second Cap was made in 1445 by Peter Wilkinson, hatter in Coney Street, for forty shillings. It was made from beaver and covered with velvet and gold lace. A third cap was made in 1579 from felt with crimson velvet, gold tassels and gold band. In 1915 George V presented the city with yet another cap, made by Anderson's the tailors, again in crimson velvet, trimmed with ermine from the robe the king had worn at his coronation.

David Wilson was born in 1931,

in the Guildhall, in the caretaker's flat above the offices. My father William James 'Jock' Wilson, was the caretaker of the Guildhall. He came there in 1925. The cook and maids lived in the Mansion House, but the butler didn't. My dad was the mace bearer when Arthur Wright was sword bearer, then later Bill Simpson [who became the butler] *was mace bearer, when Dad became the sword bearer.* [In his first year, he officiated at the visit of the Duke and Duchess of York, later to become King George VI and Queen Elizabeth, and a visit from the Prime Minister Lloyd George].

He was in charge of the Guildhall maintenance, looking after the Town Clerk and the City Engineer and the Deputy Town Clerk, and their accommodation. He had two cleaning ladies every morning, but he had to supervise everything, the boiler

Lloyd George (fourth from right) receiving the Freedom of the City, at the Mansion House 1925; Lord Mayor is Robert Newbald Kay, Jock Wilson front right with mace. (David Wilson)

Duke and Duchess of York, later King George VI and Queen Elizabeth on steps of Mansion House, 1925. Jock Wilson at front with mace. (David Wilson)

house, the heating, the council chamber. He had to put out everything in the committee room downstairs.

I used to go round to see the butler, help him wash the chandeliers in Lux and water, in the butler's pantry, dry them and put them up again. The sword and mace didn't need that much cleaning because they were silver gilt, and the sword was in its scabbard all the time.

In the flat there were two and a half bedrooms, a living room, kitchen, then a bathroom, and you went through rooms to get to it. On Armistice Sunday, I used to have to climb up the ladder and lower the flag [on the roof] *to half mast at eleven o'clock when I could hear the bugle sound in the Cenotaph.*

As a young boy, David would go fishing with his father in the river behind the Guildhall. The family also had a boat which took a lot of his leisure time, it was named Polly after his grandmother. But he also,

used to roller skate in the Guildhall. When I was nine, they put the scaffolding up, so we had to skate round it. The Guildhall was being re-roofed. And all the timber was hauled up. There was a ladder up to a hatch and I remember going up. I wasn't supposed to.

Coney Street was two way traffic, it was very pleasant. The horse and cart would come down from the railway delivering goods. I remember Potter-Kirby, who owned Kirby Nicholson's, an outfitters, [next door]. *I used to whistle at the girls in the room at the back, in fact I went out with one of them once. If you go down the Guildhall yard, you've got the garages on the left hand side, there's a building goes the full length, that was their work room, where they'd do sewing and alterations. Potter-Kirby, his door was the last door before the Mansion*

David Wilson on his boat called Polly on River Ouse 1942 (David Wilson)

Jock Wilson and son David as baby, fishing behind Guildhall (David Wilson)

David Wilson's 21st birthday at the Guildhall, 1952, with parents and girlfriend Betty, now his wife. (David Wilson)

House. He had a flat upstairs. He was a real dapper little man. He wore pinstriped trousers, a black jacket and a bowler hat.

During the war, in the basement of the Guildhall was the head-quarters of the ARP [Air Raid Precautions]. *When the raid started* [the 'Baedeker' raid in April 1942], *I was in bed, and there was a bang and I ended up on a chair in* [my sister's] *bedroom by the window. My friend Eric Walker in Blake Street, they lived upstairs and the front door was blown off and was in the middle of the road.*

We had a bell in our bedroom which was an observer alarm. It went at the same time as the siren. We had to evacuate down-stairs into the basement. We were down there and my mother

*turned to my sister and said, "Take that lad outside and show
him what's going on because he may never see it again". And
we went onto the river frontage and looked, and, opposite,
Rowntree's sugar warehouse was on fire. The Guildhall was on
fire. We were evacuated out before it got serious and into the
Mansion House. My sister was going in and a chappie put a tin
helmet on her head. And it's a good job he did, because the tin
helmet was covered in molten lead and it was all down the back
of her coat.*

*We weren't allowed down Coney Street. The church was all
destroyed. The joiners had just finished it* [the Guildhall], *brand
new vertical timbers, a brand new lead roof.*

Guildhall ruins, 1942 *(David Wilson)*

The only thing that was damaged, my mother's bedroom window, all the glass was crazed, just like a windscreen that had been smashed. It hadn't gone inside. My father had gone to hospital, he'd fallen through the roof into the roof of the assistant solicitor's offices.

Bill Simpson went to work in the Mansion House in 1934, as assistant butler and steward, graduating to butler, until he retired in 1972. He served under 28 Lord Mayors.

I'd started as a hall boy at Saltmarsh Hall. I got two pound a month and used to send thirty shillings to my mother. At the Mansion House I had to learn how to clean silver. I'd be given one fork and shown how to clean it, just one article for quite a long while. The old silver would be cleaned with 'jeweller's rouge'.

I enjoyed my time in the Mansion House. The Town Clerk, Tom Benfield, had a hard job to get me to go on my holidays. I loved the job so much. My wife said, "You're always in the Mansion House, you want to take your bed and go and sleep there". They used

Guildhall passageway
(David Wilson)

to call me 'the shadow behind the throne'. I had a staff of eight working under me, including a deputy butler, cook, kitchen maid and two housemaids. They looked after the Lord Mayor well then. The first allowance they got was in 1940, and Alderman Horsman, then Lord Mayor, got £750 which was a good sum.

Jock Wilson with sword and Bill Simpson with mace in procession at York Minster 1951. Lord Mayor is Ernest Harwood, behind him is Alderman Mrs Crichton (York's first female Lord Mayor in 1942). (David Wilson)

We had three Assizes every year and four Quarter Sessions. When the judges arrived, they'd go to the Judges lodgings. We'd go over there at night time, the Lord Mayor, the Sheriff, the Town Clerk and the Chief Constable, with the sword and mace to give them welcome to the city, and have a little drink at the same time. The following morning they'd come to the Guildhall

*to open the Assizes, then back to the Mansion House for break-
fast. It was a marvellous meal, a mixed grill, and they'd finish
up with strawberries and cream.*

*Procession to admit General Smuts to the Freedom of the City 1931. Lord Mayor Foster-
Todd, Jock Wilson at front with mace.* (David Wilson)

**When we had Quarter Sessions, Mr Minter the City Engineer,
said, "Could Mrs Simpson cook lunch for us?" There were about
40 of them that day. He went down in his car and asked her and
she was there for 18 years after that** [Bill's wife Gladys became
the Mansion House cook]. *She was a lovely cook and even got
praised by the Russian ambassador for her apple pies.*

I've met all the members of the Royal family, from Queen Mary downwards. The Duke of Windsor, formerly the Prince of Wales, the last time I looked after him was when they came to the Gentlemen's Club in Lendal. They used to have dinner there, and they were drunk as skunks. They'd use dining room chairs as sledges, coming down the stairs. It's a wonder they didn't break their legs.

The Queen Mother came for the opening of the Guildhall and had lunch in the Mansion House and I did the table decoration myself. She said, "Who does the table decoration, it's a marvellous show?" I would do all the flowers, and in the centre of the table a fountain with water running. I got that from House's [House & Son in Blake Street]. *I'd connect it up to the electric*

Launch of the author's book on Olympic Sports in York at the Mansion House
(York Archaeological Trust)

and I'd stand an old silver dish in the middle and cover it with flowers and hide the cable under. People wondered where the water was coming from.

I remember Princess Elizabeth when her father and mother were alive. They were going to Sledmere, Sir Richard Sykes's place and he rang the Lord Mayor and said, "Could we borrow Simpson? We've got the royal family coming for dinner and my butler has the willies, he's never looked after royalty". So they sent this car out to pick me up. With royalty, once you've looked after them once or twice, they never forget you. When we went to the Duke of Kent's wedding at York Minster [1961], the reception was at Hovingham. I was going through the hallway and Prince Charles said, "Oh Simpson, can you get me an ice-cream please I'm parched". And Princess Anne said, "Oh Charles, you've had three already. You'll make yourself sick".

Once we went to Westminster and this chap on the door said, "You can't go in there". I said, "I can, I'm with the Lord Mayor of York". "You're not allowed, the Lord Mayor is but you can't go in". I said, "If I don't go in there, the Lord Mayor won't be going in". Then Sir Harry Hylton-Foster who was the Speaker, came out, and he said, "Wherever the Lord Mayor goes, Simpson goes. See he gets proper attention".

I used to attend the Lord Mayor and Lady Mayoress everywhere they went. When the Lord Mayor went with the Sheriff to private dinners, I'd act as toast master. I served as toastmaster for nearly 50 years, functions all over Yorkshire. I don't think that the Lord Mayor gets the same amount of pomp and ceremony that they used to, and which they're entitled to. [Since they began to hold weddings at the Mansion House, Bill Simpson's grandson Mark Henson chose to marry Joanne Lomas in 2013 in the place so dear to his grandfather.]

John Boardman was Lord Mayor in the late 1990s and recalls some of the gifts given to the city,

Councillor John Boardman when Lord Mayor in 1996, at the launch of Van Wilson's book on Hungate, at the Archaeological Resource Centre.

We got a lot of gifts, quite a few from Norwegians who come for the Viking festival. A strange lump of rock is a carving of a lone Viking on his longboat. We were also given a hideous figure of a Madonna, a very tiny tankard which only holds about a mouthful of liquid and a bilberry harvester. Some of the furniture actually belonged to the Castle Museum including some incredibly intricately designed cabinets. There's also a chinoiserie [object of Chinese art] *in one of the store rooms, with beautiful Chinese carvings on all the sides. At least it stays cool in there and won't get marked by the sun. There's an appalling portrait of Prince Andrew and Sarah Ferguson which had been on show until things changed with them! Then it had to be hung on the back staircase and kept out of sight if any visiting royalty should come.*

The State Room has the minstrels' gallery above, where the York Waits would often perform. [Until 1835 the York Waits, minstrels, were paid a salary to perform their music for the Lord Mayor and his guests]. *There are fluted fleur de lys pillars and original chandeliers. In the dining hall the dining table has a 'starting handle'. It fits onto the end of the table to make it expand when more than 42 guests are present. Also in the dining room is a casket which was made for Winston Churchill in 1942, from the timbers of the damaged Guildhall. It contains a scroll presenting him with the honorary Freedom of the City. When he was told of this honour, he said, "Can't you put it in the post?" Too busy, I suppose! There was a ceremony in the Minster but as he never came, he never received it. A shame, as it is beautifully designed.*

The Mansion House has many treasures. The mayoral chains, which are very heavy, date from 1603. There are many items of gold and silver including the gold mace. The mace bearer carries this over his left shoulder when the Mayor goes to any official ceremonies. In the old days the mace and sword always had to precede the Mayor, even if he only went out for a packet of fags! The sword is also very heavy and beautifully decorated and inscribed from about 1672. There's also a jewelled sword, numerous goblets, dishes, pots and trophies and a 24 carat gold whistling tankard. The idea was that when you finished drinking, you turned it upside down and blew the whistle. Beside it is the silver chamber pot which also has a whistle underneath. The only silver whistling chamber pot in the city!

From the roof, where you could sunbathe in warm weather, you can see not only the whole of the city but as far as the Wolds in the distance on a good day.

Keith Hyman, Councillor of the Huntington and New Earswick ward, was the Lord Mayor in 2012–13, after having been the Sheriff in 2006. To elect each Lord Mayor,

There are 47 councillors and each councillor scores a point for their party. At the moment Labour are in charge and they've got let's say 26 councillors, they get 26 points, Conservatives have got 10 so they get 10 points, Lib Dems have got 8 points and so on. Whoever has the most points gets to appoint the Lord Mayor. Then they lose 47 points so they go onto a minus figure the next year. Next year's going to be Labour, the following year Conservative and then it will depend on the election results.

The Council Chamber in the Guildhall

(David Wilson)

In our party, you can either nominate yourself or be nominated by someone else, which is nice if you are. If there are two people, then it's a straight vote. They choose somebody and then it goes to full council in December. But it's not ratified until the annual council meeting in May. I've never seen any dissent. It's the party's choice how they want to go forward.

I think that our system's a bit fairer, spreads it round a bit. As Lord Mayor you're supposed to represent the city not yourself, so you shouldn't make any controversial statements, which I think is absolutely right. And most are pretty good at that. It's an apolitical position so I don't sit on any committees other than chair full council, about five or six times a year. You still have your ward work. The residents still get in touch. I still have to do that but I'm fortunate in that we have three councillors in our ward because it's so big. It's the residents that get me elected in the first place. I could never be Lord Mayor without them.

It's a fantastic experience. In many ways it would be good if you could be Lord Mayor early on in your career as a councillor, because you learn so much about the city as opposed to when I started, and most people start, you only know about your ward.

Keith and his wife Karen, the Lady Mayoress, have lived in the Mansion House during their year in office. They occupied the apartment on the top floor.

When we first started we did both, mainly staying at home and then coming and staying here. Then we realised there are so many events and you finish late and start early, going home was difficult. I suppose the deciding factor was my wife's wardrobe. For a man it's a lot easier. It's a suit unless it's a morning suit or black tie dinner, so it's quite easy to have enough stuff here and at home. For my wife, as Lady Mayoress, which wardrobe she was going to wear would depend on the event she was going to. So having it half at home and half of it here didn't work. I think this year especially they've noticed the Lady Mayoress and the Sheriff's Lady have dressed the part for everything they've gone to.

Sizewise the flat rooms are massive. The bedroom is two or three times bigger than our bedroom at home. But there are less rooms. The kitchen's very small, the bathroom is in need of love and attention.

Unfortunately there's no butler, no cook. There is a cleaner that comes in, it's gone down to once a week. I think the budget is pretty much the same as it was 40 odd years ago. The Lord Mayor did live in the whole of the house. We can use anywhere in the house except when it's hired out by other organisations.

With the meetings and briefings, and the events we go to, it's around 700 in the year. That's two a day most days. You don't have to go to 700 but I think to miss anything would be a waste. [At Christmas, they attended 23 carol concerts]. *I honestly don't think that most people have any idea how many a Lord Mayor goes to. During the year you're called on to speak about 300 and odd times. Between the four of us,* [the Lord Mayor, Lady Mayoress, Sheriff and his Lady] *we will go to everything we possibly can. If that means rushing from one thing to another, then we will do it. It's not possible for every Lord Mayor to do that. Some are older, and physically it's quite demanding. You can't work* [outside]. *So it tends to be an older person.*

Richard Pollitt runs the house and the staff to a certain extent. Anne Platt is the only civic support that we have. She does our diaries. When she's off it's Fiona who does bookings for here and the Guildhall. When I was Sheriff, there was Anne, and two part-timers. And we were only doing 450 events five years ago. Now we're doing 200 more and it's just Anne. The civic support officers do the driving and look after us in the house.

There is no longer a chauffeur. The Lord Mayor's car has had the number plate with registration DN1 (York's number 1 car) since the beginning.

Now it's a new DN1 [a Nillson limousine]. *They got it last April* [2012] *before the Queen got here. The old one was in the garage in bits and couldn't be put back together again. It was quite old. This one was two years old when we got it. It's an ex funeral car. A lot of people were worried about the cost of it. But actually you just go to a school when you're in it, and you'll see why you should have a car like that, for the kids. If all four of us go and a driver, and if we're taking the sword and mace, that's six of us going, we can't get into a car, you can't use taxis. Sometimes we'll be out at four or five different events. You've got to get there and back. It will last for ten years or whatever. It would cost a lot more any other way of doing it.*

I have two sets of chains. The originals are worn on royal visits, St George's Day parade, Legal Sunday when all the judges come to York, annual councils, freedom parades and a few other things, between 15 and 20 times a year. They are very delicate. The Lady Mayoress's are at least 350 years old and gold, so we have to have somebody with us as part of the insurance policy.

We wear robes to services at All Saint's Church, the guilds church, so for the guilds, we don't have sword and mace. But for the St George's Day parade, [to the Minster], *then we'll have sword and mace.*

Keith Hyman, Lord Mayor 2012–13 (Civic Office)

Keith's year as Lord Mayor was the year of York 800, (800th anniversary of York becoming a self-governing city) with even more events than usual.

It was fantastic. David Horton was last Lord Mayor, he was here for the Queen's visit. But we did come for the lunch. The Ebor Vox Choir, that started at the Minster and walked to Clifford's Tower and sang there, hundreds of people, it was absolutely bril-

liant. The Olympic flame and the Paralympic flame. Those are real highlights. And the charity work that we do. It tends to be two charities. They split the money evenly. We chose a smaller charity and a bigger charity and hope the bigger charity has bigger resources to help us actually do things. And hopefully they'll make lots of money. Another highlight was the Dean of York being installed, then for it to be a lady as well, that was very good. Because I'd been Sheriff, it did help so nothing's really been sprung on me that I didn't expect.

There are some things we do every month which actually are really good. Something called 'Citizenship' in the state room, we give UK citizenship to people by presenting them with passport forms and certificates to say they are UK residents.

They come from all over the world. Most of them have been in York for a long time. I think the longest one was 40 odd years before he decided to apply. We do on average about 30 people a month. I think the most nationalities in one time was 21 in one week. The biggest population is still Chinese, but from all parts of Africa, the USA, South America, a fair number from Nepal because of the Ghurkas and the army.

Holocaust Memorial Day, York celebrates better than many other places because of Clifford's Tower and the history there. There's a vigil with candles on the Sunday. It's always cold and wet and windy. We did an event at St John's and they actually asked me to speak at it.

The leader of the council and I met, very early on before I started, to look at economic development opportunities in the city. Obviously China is a big one. York University are having their 50th anniversary this year and also are going to Hong Kong and China to celebrate. They do degree ceremonies out there. They have strong links with Nanjing University. So we went along for four and a half days.

Historically Münster and Dijon have been York's twin cities.

Münster is still at the moment twinning, I think the new Lord Mayor will be going in July because the Yorkshire Regiment and the army are pulling out of Münster. There are still some civic events, and quite a strong Münster-York association.

Dijon is a different kettle of fish. I went with the leader of the council, one or two universities and York professionals. That was a forerunner of going to China in a way. Hopefully there will be collaborations. Lots of people want to twin with York, it's a lovely city. We've had visits from the Philippines ambassador, Cuban people, St Augustine in Florida which is the oldest town in the USA, four or five Chinese delegations. And letters from Croatia or Serbia about twinning with us. We can't do it because it all costs money.

The Mansion House is much more accessible to the public today than it was even ten years ago. There are regular visits by parties of schoolchildren.

Dan Snow was here last year doing something about medieval feasts. And they had that fantastic programme on television a couple of years ago, 'Eternal Law'. They filmed the sniper from the roof. The kitchens are used regularly. A lot of Saturday mornings you'll find people making chocolate. A local business uses it, and hen parties come and help make chocolate.

When Royalty comes, the sniffer dogs come round the Mansion House, the police check everything out. When they come to the city it's about the ceremony of the sword, the Queen has

*to touch the sword for permission to come in, then it's held
inverted until she leaves again.*

*I suppose the big thing is the change in the Lord Mayor, at one
time it was only business people who did it. But then after the
1960s, more people could have chance to be Lord Mayor of York,
it was encouraged, though not all that many people can financially do it.* [Lord Mayors are out of pocket because they do not
get paid, only an allowance.]

*Another new event is one instigated by the Friends of York Walls,
an annual inspection of the Bar Walls by the Lord Mayor, accompanied by a local primary school. Each year the Lord Mayor
selects two charities. For 2012-2013 these were Special Olympics
City of York and the Forces SSAFA. One event to raise funds was
a visit to RAF Linton on Ouse with a draw made for a flight in
the simulator. Other charity events included a Ghurka Curry
Evening in the Guildhall, with curry prepared by chefs from
the Ghurka regiment based in Fulford; George Hudson evening,
to celebrate his life with a character actor and speaker; Lord
Mayor's Golf Day, held at Pike Hills Golf Club for the sixth time;
Huge 'York's famous party band' at New Earswick Bowls Club;
Brass Band Night at the Proms; and an Oliver Cromwell raffle,
with the opportunity to win a mainline ride on the footplate of
the Oliver Cromwell preserved steam locomotive.*

Janet Pigott came to York at the age of one and stayed until she
got married.

*There was a beautiful shop in Coney Street called Border's. It
sold gorgeous-smelling coffee and it specialised in tea sales in
the shop downstairs, and upstairs there was a lovely restaurant. My Aunt Molly, Molly Pritchard, was a waitress. In 1956
and 1957 when I was taking my Pitman's, RSA, and Northern*

Counties exams in shorthand and typing, we had the afternoon off from Technical College immediately prior to the exam to help us relax. They were always called twilight exams round about five o'clock in the afternoon. So I used to go to Border's and sit at one of the tables where I knew my Aunt would be serving. I would order a pot of tea and toasted teacake, and sit quietly for a while then walk back down Coney Street to the Technical College which was in Marygate and I'd take the exam. Because I passed every time, eventually it became a ritual. I just associated it with passing. Over the two years I managed to pass the 12 certificates, ranging from Stage I to Stage III.

The job in the Guildhall was my second job, that was in 1957. I was 18. Two things that struck me particularly were the accuracy needed in our work, and the friendliness and support of the staff. Legal documents had to be pristine with no erasures. Transcriptions from shorthand had to be perfect.

When I first started, I worked for a young man called Donald Atkinson who had an office upstairs which he shared with Miss Davison. I had a desk downstairs in an office with Geoff Hall, Twiggy Leafe, Cath Ferguson (who used to drive to work every day from Whitby) and a lady called Ethel. They were great colleagues. I think there were about 22 of us on the staff. After a few weeks I was transferred to the General Office to work for Derrick Hoyle, the Committee Clerk responsible for recording the proceedings of the Housing Committee, the Grants & Loans and Building and Planning Sub Committees, and the full Council. He was a wonderful boss who typed with fury just using two fingers on each hand. He had a great sense of humour and could read my shorthand better than I could. He gave me an excellent grounding in administration and secretarial duties. When I was at Town Clerk's I used to get about £8 a week. It was just a pound a week short of what my dad got.

There was a structured salary scale for shorthand-typists and the starting rung was dependent upon age and experience. In addition to that there were increments of 2s 6d, 5s and 7s 6d for each proven qualification at RSA Levels I, II and III. I was paid monthly into a Trustee Savings Bank account.

I remember attending my first Council meeting with Derrick. He said, "If you don' t know a councillor's name don't worry about it, just jot down an obvious feature, like red hat or thick glasses. I'll know who they are when it comes to transcribing your notes." Sometimes there would be a lot of cross-talk in meetings and suddenly the Chairman would say, "Right, that's settled." And moved on to the next item on the agenda without summing up.

I did 120 words a minute. I think this is why Derrick gave me the opportunity to go with him so I could keep my shorthand speed up. After full council meetings the Minutes were printed and I had to stick a copy in the official Minutes Book, ready to be signed at the next council meeting.

One of my favourite characters was Mr Percy Cooke, the Chief Clerk and Lord Mayor's Secretary. He was a lovely man, a father figure who ran a happy ship. Very occasionally we had to man the enquiry counter at lunchtimes. One day when I was on duty, a young boy about 11 came into the office in a state of distress. He said he'd lost half-a-crown in Coney Street, it had rolled down the gutter and dropped into a drain. Someone had told him to report it to the Town Clerk's Office because he might be able to get it back when the drains were cleaned. Mr Murphy said that he didn't think that we could help, but he'd take his name and address and pass it on to the Engineer's Department. The boy burst into tears because he didn't have enough money to get home. So I got my purse out and gave him half a crown so that he could get home. Later that week Mr Cooke came to see me. He'd heard about the incident and told me never to give my own money to anybody, otherwise word would get around and all sorts of people would come in with tales about losing money. He said the drain had now been cleaned and the half crown retrieved, and he gave me a replacement coin. I felt sure the drain couldn't have been cleaned so quickly, and that it probably wasn't the boy's original coin – but I accepted it with thanks. I knew in my heart that although I'd had a mild reprimand, I also had a very kind employer looking after me.

We worked from 9 o'clock to half past five and had 1½ hours off for lunch. My friend, Frances Thompson, used to cycle all the way home to Mellwood Grove in Beckfield Lane for lunch. When we suggested she brought sandwiches she was horrified

Mansion House 1950s (David Wilson)

*and said she liked the exercise. There was a young office boy
cum clerk, over six foot tall, Peter Harrison, he left to go to
RADA. I once saw him in a television play and he'd changed his
name to Peter York.*

*There were no computers. Word processors weren't invented
until 1964, and the first ones cost thousands of pounds. There
was no email or internet or spell-check facilities. There were
comptometers and punched card systems for mathematical
calculations, but no spreadsheets and modern day technology.
Telephone systems were either peg boards or plug boards. There
was no Direct Dialling. All calls had to be made through an
operator at the telephone switchboard or exchange. There were
no mobile phones. I don't know what today's people would do.*

*Tape recorders were large
and cumbersome and had
spools of magnetic tape
for recording the spoken
voice. There were also
Emidicta machines where
the voice was recorded
onto a gramophone record,
but it was impossible to
back-track and re-listen to
misheard words or phrases.
We relied on the accu-
racy of shorthand. All the
typewriters were manuals
in the '50s and '60s. Office
work could be very noisy if*

*Janet Pigott and Frances Thompson,
1950s (Janet Pigott)*

half a dozen or so were clattering away at the same time. There were no typing chairs with five feet and casters. All our typing chairs had three feet. Health and Safety regulations weren't in force. Paper sizes were also different. We typed letters on quarto and foolscap paper and took carbon copies because there were no photocopying machines. The Liverpool Exchange Member of Parliament, Bessie Braddock, used to write to the Town Clerk on pink paper, using the red part of a bichrome typewriter ribbon, and sign her letters in red ink, because she was Labour. The Town Clerk always replied in black print on white paper. He was T C Benfield, Derrick called him Tom. That's another thing, formality is out now. It was always Miss or Mr or Mrs. I was Miss Taylor.

There was no such thing as white correcting fluid. If anybody made a mistake, if it was a legal document, it had to be re-typed. If you were doing a letter to somebody, and it didn't contain anything legal, we were allowed to use a proper typing rubber.

At one time, a film crew came. All of the admin staff were asked to sit up in the public gallery [of the council chamber]. *They took a film of a mock council meeting. We were given instructions that we were supposed to laugh at certain times, or look aghast. And Derrick was supposed to be so unconcerned, he was reading a newspaper. When we came to see this film, you couldn't see Derrick, only the newspaper.*

One of the nicest things that happened was when the Queen came and the Town Clerk paid privately for his staff to have an identical meal the next day as a thank you to them all, whilst all the flowers and the name cards were still in place. That was a real treat for us.

Once the Queen Mother was due to visit the city and sent her personal mother-of-pearl toilet seat on in advance, to be fixed for her use whilst she was on her visit. Mr Simpson, the Lord Mayor's butler, who was normally very serious, straight-laced and aloof, was amused by this request and told us about it. He invited all the ladies to come and look at it and we each took turns in sitting on it for a moment or two. Thank goodness she never knew, otherwise we might have all been in trouble.

One of the scariest things that happened was that Tom Atkinson, the mace bearer and caretaker, once showed us a secret door in the oak panelling of the Committee room. It led to a priest hole, with a flight of steps down to a landing at the side of the River Ouse. Two or three of us would use it in our lunch-times in the hot summer days and go for a swim in the river. But one day the water was particularly oily and we had to clean up in a wash basin in the toilets.

Staff from Guildhall swimming behind the Guildhall (David Wilson)

I was the last to get washed, and as I bent down and switched the gas water heater on, the pilot light back-fired and my hair caught alight. The crackling noise came first and the acrid smell made me stand up instantly. Through the mirror I could see the crown of my head aflame. I grabbed my towel and threw it over my head to quell the flames. After that I never went swimming in the Ouse again.

Geoff Hattersley was the Lord Mayor's chauffeur and he used to come into the Town Clerk's office while he was waiting. I remember going in there when Princess Margaret got married. The City of York had made a wedding present for her, a silver cockerel. I thought, "What on earth is she going to do with it?" The York City silversmiths had made it.

The judges would come when it was Assize court time and stay in the Judges' House in Lendal. And it was custom and practice to give them a silver snuff box as a thank you for coming. Derrick would go across to Hopper's jewellers and choose it.

It was a job that I enjoyed very much indeed and it gave me a fantastic start to my working life. I got married in 1961 and moved away.

Suzy Brown went to work at the Guildhall in 1969 as a shorthand typist.

The typewriters were the old fashioned type, black with keys having to be pushed down about 2" to type out a letter or a document or minutes. I worked in the legal department and with the committee clerks. The work was exceptionally interesting and you did find out first hand a lot of the agreements that would be made to do with the city of York. I did the typing up of legal documents on proper parchment. That's when you really couldn't make mistakes.

When there was anything ceremonial happening at the Mansion House, I helped with the arrangements. The Lord Mayor's secretary at the time liked my style of handwriting and when the Queen and Prince Philip came to York to the 1971 celebrations of the founding of the city, she asked me to do all the name place cards for the luncheon to be held at the Assembly Rooms, along with the table plan. Many of us were chosen to be at one of the functions at which the Queen attended. I was fortunate to be chosen to have luncheon in the Assembly Rooms. Someone had forgotten the seating plan for the afternoon tea in the Museum Gardens, so I was asked to take it along there and was given a badge to wear so that I could enter. The Duke of Edinburgh stopped me on my way to the marquee and asked me about my

Suzy Grey on right, and Mavis Bell at Mansion House, 1969 (Suzy Brown)

badge. *I was quite taken aback and the only thing that came in to my head was to say, "It's my passport into here". He laughed and went on his way.*

The staff were a lot older. It was mainly men that were the committee clerks. The electoral registration was at the other side of the building. That was a really interesting place. And it was in May when they did the votes, it was a day off work and extra pay. I just sat in the Guildhall but you could go to any of the polling stations.

I don't think you had so many timescales. You were there to do a job and you did it in that day. You didn't do overtime, it wasn't necessary. I'm from the old school, people send emails, I find it atrocious that people don't even read through them. The typing errors and spelling mistakes! When we were training to be typists we would have speed tests. If you had ten mistakes that would be taken off the time. So if you typed 50 words a minute, if you had ten mistakes, it would take it down to 40 words. It's gone, accuracy, grammar, and now with texting, people shorten words. I don't think people are conscientious anymore. It's not taught.

I enjoyed the job. We were totally involved in most of what was going on, or we knew about it. It was the hub of the city of York. It was nice to go to work every day.

Another offshoot is the Guildhall Orchestra which formed in 1980, and is in its 33rd season in 2013. The orchestra initially performed at the Guildhall and occasionally the Minster and eventually the Barbican Centre. The orchestra usually performs three times a year. It was founded by John Hastie, director of music at Bootham School, and Simon Wright became conductor in 1992. It is now the official orchestra of the City of York.

— *Chapter 3* —
LEAK *and* THORP

Leak and Thorp in 1920s (Ian Collinson)

Leak and Thorp began its life in 1848 in Parliament Street, as a general draper's, at first named Leak and Holme. William Leak wrote in his ledger on his first day that he opened the store 'with fear and trembling'.

An early advertisement promises,
Messrs Leak and Holme propose attending the London and Manchester markets regularly buying goods, and hope, by their experience in business, that their establishment may not be excelled by any other House.

As the business developed, the shop extended into the adjoining building and the number of young male employees increased from three to ten. One of these was Vernon Wragge, who became Lord

Mayor of the city thirty years later. The named changed again, to William Leak and Co, but by 1855 its final name was Leak and Thorp, when Mr H Thorp joined, along with John Booth and Samuel Wright.

Within a few years the business needed bigger premises and when the George Inn on Coney Street came onto the market, it proved to be the perfect site. On 3rd April 1869, the company announced its grand opening. The goods on offer included *'an extensive assortment of muslin, lace and leno curtains, French printed muslin grenadines, and a new department for children's clothes. Gentlemen's clothes include fancy trowserings and vestings'*.

The shop was four storeys high and 84 feet long, with six show windows, each 14 feet high, protected by patent iron shutters. Adjoining it were a counting house, private office and parcels room. The office was well lit with large skylights in the centre, and fitted with mahogany and black ebony. A grand staircase led to the first floor showroom. Behind this was the dining hall and domestic office. The third floor was divided into living accommodation for the assistants, which included a young men's library, young ladies' sitting room, bedrooms and bathrooms. The fourth floor also housed bedrooms. Another staircase on the ground floor led down to the basement and the carpet showroom. The premises were heated by 'hot water batteries'. The number of staff had greatly increased and assistants were graded into first sales, second sales and the lowly third sales.

Soon the store was attracting a wide range of clientele, including the local gentry. An account dated 1876 for Miss Cholmley of Brandsby Hall includes haberdashery items (two packets of pins, eight reels, ribbon, 8 dozen buttons) as well as crepe cloth, braid and lining, seven pairs of gloves and seven bonnets coming to a total of £15.

In 1884 William Leak became Sheriff of York and eight years later an additional block was added to the store which seemed to be concentrating on 'Turkey, Persian and Indian carpets, hearth rugs, linoleums and floor cloths for entrance halls, offices and public rooms. Spring, hair, wool and straw mattresses, feathers, curled hair, flocks, quilts, sheetings, blankets, table and household linen'.

Early drawing of Leak and Thorp 1893 (B Antoni)

But in 1899 fashion became more prominent and included many exclusive designs, with costumes tailor-made by expert cutters and fitters. The shop advertised,

The latest novelties for the present season, with ladies' mantles, jackets, capes, plain and braided tailor made costumes, waterproofs, cycling jackets. Ladies shirts, blouses, sunshades, chiffons, lace scarfs. Dress and costume materials in all the newest productions, voiles, embroidered robes in various tints, striped taffeta silks, rich black brocades, navy and white foulards. Newest French models in millinery, bonnets, sailor and walking hats. Flowers and feathers in great profusion. Ladies tea gowns, silk foundations and under-clothing. Children's costumes and coats in new French shape. Tweeds for gents and boys suits, coats, hats and caps, shirts, collars, cuffs, ties. Travelling trunks, portmanteaus, hat cases, bonnet boxes, Gladstone bags.

Horse and cart from Leak and Thorp (Ian Collinson)

In 1905, Leak and Thorp was converted into a private limited company, with capital of £65,000, and registered as general drapers, silk mercers, milliners, dress and mantle makers, woollen drapers and tailors, carpet warehousemen and general furnishers.

The directors were Samuel Wright, John Booth, William Wright, Samuel Wright junior and Thomas Booth. Samuel Wright was also a Methodist lay preacher and philanthropist, and three times Sheriff of York. He went to Buckingham Palace to personally present an album of watercolours of York to Queen Victoria. Booth and Wright led the firm for 40 years.

William Collinson, who would play a large part in the history of Leak and Thorp, joined the business in 1908, and was joined in 1911 by Arthur Audsley, who went on to serve in the First World War, was

Leak and Thorp van 1918. Driver John Kendall (Ian Collinson)

invalided out and rejoined the firm in 1919 as buyer for fabrics and household linens. He stayed there until retirement in 1960.

A letter to Mr Railton in October 1910, is an example of an offer of a job in the store.

'Referring to your call respecting the vacancy in one of our cash desks, we beg to say that we have decided to favour your application, and we shall be glad if you will arrange to take up your duties on Monday the 10th instant at 8.30am. It is agreed that commencing wage shall be 3s per week, with food and 6d extra if cash balances throughout the week'. (Which suggests that sometimes it might not!!)

In January 1911 there was an installation of a new shop front by Frederick Sage & Company of London. The press reported that, *'Third class fares will be paid to all purchasers of parcels of £5 and upwards within a radius of 50 miles'.*

A few months later the store became the agency for the three-guinea Burberry coat, which joined the top coats, suits, gowns, hats, motoring

Seamstresses at Leak and Thorp 1884. Head seamstress Elizabeth Laihy
(Ian Collinson)

William Collinson, 1931
(Ian Collinson)

Facing page: Leak and Thorp football team, winners of half-holiday league 1911–12. Back row: Thompson, Hood, Murphy, Andrews, Wragg, Smith. Standing in coats: J Young, captain, F Healey, secretary. Middle row: J Thompson, Nickson, Rafton, Pollard, Wilson. Front row: Smedley, Roberts, Taylor.
(Ian Collinson)

Leak and Thorp very early years (Ian Collinson)

and riding kits. In September 1912, dress materials included Cumberland and Airedale tweeds, admiralty serges and velveteens. Men's overcoats in frieze and nap cloths were 30s, and Dexter weatherproofs 'for gentlemen and gentlewomen' were ready to wear at 30s and made to measure at 50s. The firm declared *'we live in an age when men are often summed up at a glance. Don't let faulty attire stand between you and achievement'*.

During the First World War, Leak and Thorp had to make changes to ensure sales continued. It kept up a weekly half page advertisement in the Yorkshire Evening Press. In the summer of 1914, there was a big window display of trunks, bags and suitcases. As travelling for pleasure lessened, these were probably aimed at soldiers leaving the city. By the autumn the shop was selling *'a large stock of black dress materials suitable for family mourning. Families waited on at shortest notice. Telephone day or night'*.

The Christmas 1914 advertisement, as well as offering the usual range of goods, such as *'hundreds of toys from 1d, satin slippers at 1/11½d and afternoon tea cloths at 4/11d to 15s'*, there were also gifts available for loved ones in the army, khaki mufflers, khaki wool mitts, natural wool body belts, jackets, wool helmets and worsted half-hose. Two years later the firm branched out to become funeral directors.

In the 1920s, William Collinson succeeded Samuel Wright as Secretary and more goods were being imported, such as *'Eastern silks at exceptional value. Natural shantung, Ninghai silks, Fugi, Schappe, ivory Japanese satin, natural Pongee silks'*.

In 1929 the firm held its diamond jubilee. From humble beginnings and a small turnover, the number of staff had increased to 150. To mark the occasion, the firm offered 10 per cent discount for all cash purchases during three days in April, and also held a staff outing with three coaches.

Coach outing for staff, 1920s (Ian Collinson)

In 1932 the rooms on the third floor which had been used by male staff were converted into a café. There were chaise longues for ladies to rest on in the fashion department. A new form of cash registering, the pneumatic tube system, was installed 'at considerable expense'. The oldest employee at this time was George Douglas aged 74, who had bcen there 37 years.

Unfortunately, only a year later, in January 1933, came the big fire, which started in the tailoring showroom. The headlines read 'Great drapery store a pile of ruins'. Leak and Thorp was razed to the ground, and the damage estimated at £150,000, although in the women's mantle department, wardrobes containing women's cloaks and mantles were untouched. One million gallons of water poured onto the burning premises, as the firemen, using 9,000 feet of hose, worked for eight hours. The street was closed to traffic.

Fire at Leak and Thorp, 1933 (Ian Collinson)

A *Yorkshire Herald* reporter in the neighbouring offices had noticed the smoke and rang the fire brigade. Soon four fire engines arrived and they saved Coney Street from what could have been an even greater disaster. 20 shop assistants had been on the premises but got out safely. The shop had begun a complete modernisation only a few months earlier, with a frontage of plate glass and arcades. The fire devastated W H Smith's next door, and also scorched Eycott, gown specialist, Singer, the sewing machine firm, Darling, Wood and Anfield, watch and clock makers, Thomas Cook, the tourist agency, and Johnson Bros, dyers. It was claimed that the fire could be seen as far away as Leeds.

The girls who lived on the premises were given help towards clothes and fares homes, but they all lost their jobs and some of their possessions. They told reporters that they were concerned about the welfare of the two store cats, Spats and Teddy, who disappeared and were never seen again. Leak and Thorp took a temporary office in the Herald Printing Works and later a shop in Lendal.

Maids and assistants at Leak and Thorp c.1920 (Ian Collinson)

At 10am on 27th September 1934 the new Leak and Thorp opened, an imposing steel-framed and fireproof building with a façade of white imitation Portland stone, with a double front and three arcades. The joint managing directors were now William Collinson and Arthur Audsley, other directors being T. Booth and William Birch (whose firm rebuilt the store). Inside were two electric lifts, and the ground floor housed fabrics and haberdashery, soft furnishings and household linens. In the centre were gloves, hosiery, toilet goods and perfumery, and the men's department. On the first floor was the fashion salon for women and children. The second floor housed china, glassware and hardware, with the café overlooking the river. The plan was to have a roof garden with trellis work and rambler roses. Employees were no longer resident in the building. Robert and Norman Collinson, sons of William, had joined the firm and became directors in 1938. In 1936 the store opened a hairdressing salon.

In 1937 the store led the city in its displays of flowers and flags for the coronation of King George VI. In 1948 Leak and Thorp had its centenary and celebrated on 11th March with a grand display of costumes through the ages, up to Christian Dior's New Look. Many of the exhibits came from the Kirk (now Castle) Museum.

York Chamber of Commerce, 1937. Back row: Arthur Audsley, Mrs Collinson, William Collinson, Mrs Audsley. Front row: Lord Mayor, Lady Mayoress, Sheriff and Sheriff's Lady.
(Ian Collinson)

In 1955 Leak and Thorp was innovative again when it held the first all male fashion parade in a York store. The show was compered by Norman Collinson and featured suits, sports blazers and flannels, Donegal tweeds, doeskin waistcoats, shooting sticks, sweaters and cravats. The business was going from strength to strength and in December 1959 even the Princess Royal came to do some Christmas shopping. Her connection with the city had begun when she came in 1950 to open Princess Mary Court in the Castle Museum, which featured a number of old York shops including the drapers', Leak and Holme.

Lingerie display, 1950s (Ian Collinson)

In March 1963 the store held a five-day exhibition which attracted thousands. There were demonstrations of weaving on a hand loom, glove making, tatting, knitting, and crocheting. New fabrics were on display, with experts on hand to give advice, including a fashion advisor from Vogue Patterns. In the cafe there were beauty and make-up demonstrations, and a display of lingerie, '7 Steps to Loveliness'. In the basement there were demonstrations of new pressure cookers and coffee percolators, and competitions for children. But it was in 1964 that the shop was brought even more up to date with a new shop front and canopy, new heating and lighting and a new look throughout the store. The single entrance replaced the three previous doorways. Also that year, the Council repealed the Order which had limited the opening hours of York shops, and insisted they have half day closing on Wednesday or Saturday. Leak and Thorp was one of the five York stores to open five full days. Their closing day became

Men's fashion parade (Ian Collinson)

Leak and Holme shop front in York Castle Museum (Ian Collinson)

Monday 'because it was wash day when few housewives go shopping'. They were also allowed to stay open to 8pm on Fridays. In 1969, the store celebrated 100 years in Coney Street. The Lord Mayor, Mona Armitage, unveiled the plaque to the George Inn, which still exists, and cut the cake, which was decorated with a coach and four. But there was sadness at the death of William Collinson in July 1968 at the age of 93. He had spent 65 years in the drapery trade, 45 of them at Leak and Thorp. He had recalled that in his day frock coats and silk hats were standard wear for buyers and managers, but after the First World War this gave way to lounge suits.

Even bigger changes came during 1969 when an entire new top floor was built onto the flat roof, making it the tallest shop on Coney Street. The new restaurant on the top floor was named the Norseman and opened in February 1970, seating 160, with the floor below becoming the furnishing department. The top storey also housed directors' offices, admin offices, training room, staff room, cloakrooms and a sick bay. The new 'hot air dryers' were available in the public washrooms.

Leak and Thorp anniversary cake, 1969

(Ian Collinson)

Christmas at Leak and Thorp, 1968

(Ian Collinson)

The second stage of these renovations was completed in 1970, with a new furnishings department. To complement the store's imposing presence on Coney Street, the directors decided to have an impressive Christmas display on the front of the store, which continued for several years, and which was talked about throughout York.

William Collinson, 1960s

(Ian Collinson)

Beauty parade 1960s (Ian Collinson)

One thing which was true of Leak and Thorp was the loyalty of staff. In the 1960s and '70s there were many presentations to those who had been there for 25 years or more. Two ladies had given 101 years service between them, Mabel Pinder in the millinery department and Evelyn Douglas in soft furnishings. Miss Douglas recalled that during her apprenticeship she had learnt to make shrouds and coffin linings. In 1971 Henry Kidd was presented with a floral painting and gift token for 50 years service, and was still working there at 74. He recalled sleeping on the top floor as a young man.

Robert Collinson retired as Chairman of Leak and Thorp in January 1970 (and died in August 1982 aged 77). In 1973 the shop announced that its final stage of 'a nine year modernisation plan' was completed when the store became open plan. Norman retired as Chairman in 1974, succeeded by Allen White, but continued as consultant director. He died aged 73 in 1984. But the business had already been sold, in 1981.

Leak and Thorp van 1950s (Ian Collinson)

Eileen Dickenson, who lived in the country, started work in the office of Leak and Thorp in 1946.

It was my first job from the Day School of Commerce. I had to cycle five miles to a place called Alne, leave the bicycle, walk to Alne Cross, a quarter of a mile, and catch the bus to York. It was a long day, especially in winter and that bad winter in 1947.

We weren't allowed through the front door to get to the office. We had to go down to a little door [down the lane at the side] *and the Evening Press office was down there. There was a doorman, he helped packing things in the basement area. We would either walk up the stairs or you could get the lift right up to the second floor.*

I worked with two lady clerks sat near a window. If anybody wanted to pay a bill, they would come to that window. Then later on because business got a bit better, they got a typist clerk, just to type.

Leak and Thorp waitresses

There was Mr William Collinson, the senior one. He looked about 100 and I think it would be a bow tie he had. He could get a back way into the office from his big room. He'd say, "Would you mind coming to take some shorthand please?", then I'd type it up. It would be Underwood typewriters, probably Imperials as well.

A few months after I went there, they said, "We'd like you to do the switchboard". So I had to answer all the calls, put them through to departments. Mr Rob Collinson had to go through our office, he just had an office with a glass boarding. He'd leave the door open all day long and chat to us. We had a bit of a password that if his father was coming through the other door, we had to say it so that he'd get on with his work. After a few months Mr Rob said, "I'd like you to type the cheques out. Just give it a try". And I did do, and I didn't make a mistake. Every night when I left to catch the bus in Exhibition Square I was given the post and I had to take it into the main post office in Lendal. There was tons.

He was a jolly man was Mr Rob. He called me Jennifer. "It suits you better than Eileen". Mr Norman Collinson had been wounded in the navy. He was a very nice man and I think he became something to do with the Chamber of Trade [William, Norman and Rob had all been president].

The café was fairly popular, especially when they could look out onto the river, quite a big café. We could get a meal there, we had to sit away from the rest of the customers. And then the chef, I think he was French, was getting to the end of this big tub of ice cream, and he said, "I can't scratch anymore out of here. So you two girls (the clerk and me), will you take it up on the roof and I'll give you two spoons". We took it up there because it was summer. There were spindly stairs, it was almost like walking to the top of the Minster.

Mr Audsley used to have this little office, more like a store room, a little window in it, and he'd look out to see if anybody was picking clothes up and going off with them. He was the one who watched everything.

The thing that I found a bit funny, one of the clerks told me that Lady So and So would come to the counter and say, "I've brought this dress back". I said, "Why is she bringing it back, doesn't she like it?" "No, they just want it for the night, for the ball, then they bring it back and we send it to the cleaners and it's sold in the sales".

Clothes rationing continued in England until 1949.

> *You only had so many coupons. I was a real country girl, as fit as a flea and didn't feel the cold. So in winter, because I'd no more coupons left, I'd just go in bare legs. No women wore trousers in those days apart from uniform. So my dad said, "For goodness sake I'll give you some of my clothing coupons and buy yourself some stockings".*

> *It was known as the best store, better than Brown's. If anybody had money they would go to Leak and Thorp in preference.*

Gill Fox worked at Leak and Thorp

> *as a Saturday girl between 1955 and 1957 then fulltime as a secretary 1957 to about 1959. My mother Emily Ayre worked there from the late 1940s until she retired. She was in the end the buyer for jewellery, knitting wools and needlework. She was a good friend of Mr Norman Collinson. They were Methodists, and they liked music.*

> *When I was working Saturdays they had a sale of towels and I had to pin on all the sale tickets. I remember the Director Mr Audsley showing me how to thread the pins through so they didn't prick anybody's fingers. I do remember I went to count the wool for my mother for stocktaking which I hated. And I was in a steel container that absolutely reeked of mothballs, counting the balls of wool. It was quite claustrophobic. It wouldn't be allowed now.*

> *You went through the main doors and on the right hand side was the big gents' department, selling very upmarket clothing, all run by men. Then the haberdashery store with rows and rows of buttons. People made their own clothes or had dressmakers.*

Restaurant, 1930s (Ian Collinson)

Then my mother's department with the jewellery in a big glass case, then the knitting wools and the needlework behind.

It was an L-shaped building. And at the back there was a very big fabric department, selling really beautiful and expensive fabrics. On the first floor was the hat department, shoe department and a big department of ladies fashions, ball dresses, fur and everything. Some of the fashion labels are still around now, like Dorita. All the accessories were quite upmarket.

Then another staircase, and you came up into a big furniture department and the big café restaurant with the waitresses all in black with white caps and white pinafores. There was a suite of offices, a big boardroom, oak panelled, Mr Norman's office, Mr Rob's office, and Mr Thompson, the personnel officer. And the counter for enquiries and the general office which is where

Emily Ayre with Norman and Robert Collinson (Gill Fox)

I was. The shop had a sort of coffee coloured paper and paper bags, with dark brown 'Leak and Thorp' on them. There was an old switchboard which I used to operate, with a wind up handle and plugs for each department.

It was quite Dickensian, a formal place. On either side of the main door, behind the counter were Mrs Johnson and Queenie, they sat on very high chairs with a fixed wooden shelf in front of them and huge ledgers, at least over a metre wide when they were open. All hand written, with pen and ink. Most of the regular customers had accounts. More casual customers paid in cash. In the cash office, the cash came up in little metal canisters through chutes. We took the bill out and put the change in and put it back down the chute. If a canister went astray which sometimes they did in the machinery, the people below would flap on the lids to show us that they were waiting. But shopping was a leisurely affair in those days. Nobody was rushing. There were always chairs by the glass counters for people to sit on.

I do remember typing some very archaic indentures for the hair-dressers. They had to be typed on parchment and tied up with ribbons. People had to pay to have their daughters indentured there. Norman was a very sweet man. He was the man I worked for. I think Barbara did the stuff for Mr Rob. I used to go for Mr Norman's tea which was very frightening. Behind the steel doors and the finery and white napery and everything, it was like chaos. A lot of the waitresses could swear like troopers and the chef was a figure of terror to me. Mr Norman used to want extra butter on his teacakes and I hardly dare ask for it. It was very intimidating behind those doors.

There was a window dresser, Mr Wilkinson, who was a friend of my mother's. He was quite a character, always immaculate, well-

Lower ground floor, Leak and Thorp, 1964 (Ian Collinson)

dressed and handsome. He liked to sew tapestry. Mr Audsley was a very intimidating old man and there was another old man in the towels. The cosmetic ladies were always a bit more glamorous and considered to be a little bit flighty. There was Miss Appleton who sold the shoes who was very prim and proper.

Once a week, sometimes I was allowed to help write it, we did a column for the Press of the latest things that were in the store. And Mr Norman would take it over to the Press office which was next door.

Most of the customers were known and the buyers did buy things in especially for them. Most of my wages went because they'd got something nice in that I would like. I would buy a lot of fabric there, I used to sew a lot, they would order the couture patterns for you.

There was a big social life in York. All these business people went to balls in the Assembly Rooms and they would all dress up. The draper's ball once a year was a very glamorous affair. My mother went. She looked absolutely fabulous in her fur wrap and her gown and jewellery. She had a connection with the House of Worth, I think she went once to Paris but mostly to London. It was very beautiful stuff that she bought. Dealers would come in to see her. My nephews and nieces modelled some knitted jumpers from my mother's department. They paraded up and down in the café.

My mother had a very good friend there, Miss Weatherall who was the buyer in fashions. They put on fashion shows at some of the big country houses. I remember my mother going out to where the Halifaxes lived. They were big ticketed events for York's minor aristocrats, they raised money for charitable events. They supported an orphanage on Tadcaster Road.

That was an expensive street, Coney Street, that was <u>the</u> shopping place.

June Dandy joined the Leak and Thorp hairdressing salon in 1942.

I went straight from school. I saw Mr William Collinson, the chairman, I went into his big office with my mother. There was a premium to pay but he said, "Only put half of it down first because we'll see how your daughter likes hairdressing". [Because it was wartime] *my mother said, "You won't be closing it will you?" He said, "Oh I think ladies always want their hair doing". I started at 5s a week. You had to pay a stamp of 4d. So I got 4/8d for three years.*

When you got to be apprentices, we could go up on the roof and take our towels to dry. We'd often trip up there and watch the parades coming along Coney Street. There was the manageress, Miss Nightingale and a stylist and hairdresser Maisie Lunn. But she went into the land army. You were apprentice for three years and two years improver.

I'd been there just over a week and we had the Blitz on York. I was on my cycle and I got to St Helen's Square and there was glass all over. I was carrying my bike most of the way along Coney Street. The church next door had been hit and then it was the other big arcade. They'd had firewatchers. They had to do firewatching, the senior staff. They'd been watching the incendiary bombs fall.

It was a big department. It had 12 cubicles, a beauty room and two manicure tables in a recess, very quiet, sedate. There was a hairdressing place at the other side, Grace and Hardy. And they were bombed out. So they asked our directors if they could share our salon until they got a place in Stonegate. I remember Mr

June Dandy on left (June Dandy)

Collinson saying, "Just watch our clients, see they don't go over there". We used to go upstairs for coffees for clients. The times I ran up and down those stairs. I got to hate my name. They used to say, "Where's that Miss Newby?" Because you did everything.

By 1948, '49, things were starting to improve after the war. They were having a fashion parade. Miss Nightingale had left and we had a manager, Mr Gill. Trufitt and Hill, the Bond Street firm, had a perm called Pizam and they wanted to get it started in York. It was a new type of perm, machine-less. They had a demonstration. So they wanted models. Mr Norman had said, "Why doesn't Miss Newby be a model?" "Oh no, I couldn't do that". "I tell you what might interest her. We're getting new evening dresses in and there's a lovely one just come in". It was deep purple or burgundy. So the buyer from the gown depart-ment came and brought this beautiful dress. I said, "Right", just to wear the dress. It wasn't a stage, you just walked round casually.

I became an improver, but left and went to work in Binns in Darlington.

After a few years, June came back.

There was a Mrs Wright, she was expecting her first baby. I remember her coming to have what we called' strung up to the ceiling', machine perms. I could see she was heavily pregnant. I said, "When is it expected?" She said, "Today". I said, "We'd better get it started then". I liked it at Leak and Thorp, I was there for 18 years. The previous manageress had left and Brenda Kirby came from Swallow and Barry. That upset the staff because one of the girls had put in for the job but one of the directors, Mr Audsley, had found her smoking. (That had caused the fire years ago). It was banned. If you were caught on the premises you were out straightaway. With private cubicles, it was easy for them to sneak away and have a cigarette.

Then Brenda got pregnant so she had to be off so I got made manageress. We hadn't a receptionist or a proper washing machine. So they let me have a Bendix, they let me have a cleaner, they let me have a receptionist. Things were changing and the open salons were coming in. The travellers that came from a Leeds firm, one I knew very well, Mr Waudby. He said, "Have you thought of having an open salon?" I said, "My clients wouldn't have an open salon. They like the privacy". He said, "Well it's coming". Mr Norman was all for it.

June wanted

to keep ten cubicles down one side and then an open salon in silver grey and dusky pink. They designed and put the colours in, with four backward wash basins all in pink, and a background was what you could wipe down, a lighter grey with a motif of flowers. And six dressing tables. It was all in lovely shades of pink.

We did a big demonstration. Superla came. It was done on a stand, the actual perm. They came into the gown department and the buyer was furious, they took up so much of her floor. Then they modelled. We had an afternoon and an evening, people had to have tickets. Then we had another show at the Rialto, and we went to the gas showrooms and had a bit of a do there.

As manageress, June got a new contract of employment in 1963. Her salary was £836 plus commission on the takings. In 1971 this had gone up to £915.60 per annum. She had 17 days holiday. There was no definite sick pay but the company paid for individual membership of the Private Patients' Plan.

We kept all the cubicles down one side. The beauty salon wasn't doing very much at all. It was a fairly big room so they put an extra basin in and a curtain across so the other part was the open salon. We must have had about 12 years. Then they cut it down. So instead of 12 people working for me, we'd have just about three and two juniors. Then they decided, "We think we're going to close it", after three years.

Norman retired just before the hairdressing went, he said, "Will you still cut my hair for me? Come one evening and we'll have a glass of sherry". And he'd talk about the old times, used to have me enthralled.

When she left in 1974, many of the big hairdressing salons in the city wanted June, but in the end she decided to open her own business,

The Regency near Bootham Bar, I was there for 17 years.

But she did love her time at Leak and Thorp.

I wouldn't say they were the best for paying the top wages but they were a nice firm to work for. It was a nice atmosphere.

When I look back to the way I started, in those days you wore a hat and gloves. I was so shy and timid, and the shop was so big. If anybody had said, "In years to come, you'll be the manageress", I would have taken flight. You just don't know what's round the corner.

Ian Collinson was the last family member to work at Leak and Thorp before it was taken over.

After the fire in 1933, there was a question as to whether Leak and Thorp was finished, end of story. They did reopen, it presumably meant borrowing money to do just that and they were tight for cash. The new building was done by William Birch's who still are around in York. My destiny was to become a chartered accountant which I succeeded in doing. I qualified in York and went to work in London. Really I had no intention of being involved with Leak and Thorp. My father didn't encourage me. But circumstances altered and I did come back to York and spent 20 years there until the business was taken over in 1981 by Joplings who had a department store in Sunderland. I had about 140 staff under my control when we actually finished.

At that stage the Collinson family had a controlling interest in the business. Rob was my father, Norman was my uncle, they were joint managing directors. When Joplings took over I remained as a director until such time as we parted company. A lot of the work that I'd formerly been involved with, had moved up and was taken over by the operation in Sunderland.

We shared a joint yard at the back with the Yorkshire Evening Press. There was a lot of activity. We also had two warehouses, one in Swinegate and one in Tower Street. Most of our furniture was taken there before coming up to Coney Street. There was an increasing difficulty in getting access because of restrictions on vehicles. Generally we had one van until towards the end we had two vans, one van for the carpet fitters. The deliveries at one stage were sub-contracted to another local carrier.

Leak and Thorp van 1970s (Ian Collinson)

In 1952, ten years after the clock outside St Martin's Church had been damaged, the City Engineer Charles Minter wrote to William Collinson giving approval for a clock on the front of Leak and Thorp. This had gone by the 1960s and Norman was also *instrumental in wanting to get the clock back onto St Martin's. He was very friendly with Charles Minter. It took some time to get that clock back, it's a pretty heavy object. They closed Coney Street while they had heavy lifting gear to get it back up.*

The main change [in Ian's time] *was that we put a new floor on top of the building. The lift motor room, the mechanics for the lift, were accessible from the roof so if there was a problem, we had to climb the ladders and get on the top of the building.*

Retailing was changing in those days. We were going into the business of franchises where operators would come in and take some floor space. That was quite a good situation. You can be subject to the vagaries of the weather, the changes in fashion, the length of the garment has altered and so on. If you finish a season in the fashion business, and the weather's been bad and you're left with stock, difficult to sell once the season's over. There's all kinds of hazards. If you've got an operator in on a franchise, the return on your floor space was guaranteed. If you'd got a really good arrangement, you'd got guaranteed return on your floor space and probably a share in the profits.

But sadly Leak and Thorp was sold and the York store went forever. In 1987 the large London toy shop Hamley's opened a branch in that store. Although popular, it did not prove to be as successful as hoped and closed within a year, with the loss of 34 jobs. Today the site is split into several shops, Next, Monsoon and River Island.

Leak and Thorp is a prime example of the department store which came into being in the mid 19th century. At the time, it was a great innovation. The industrial revolution and the revolution in transport and a sudden exuberance of items on offer led to the emergence of a new clientele. Upper class women who had little to do but take tea and entertain in their salons now discovered shopping. They could

It's a Bride's World

ON OUR
FASHION
FLOOR

The subtle sheen of satin,
the flattery of lace and shimmering organza—
Wedding dresses in all these can be portrayed by
our own model especially for you.
Head-dresses and veils for the Bride and Brides-
maids and flowers in profusion.
Visit the fashion floor

Leak and Thorp LTD

CONEY STREET — YORK — TEL. 58555

Bridal advert 1967 (York and County Times)

visit, without chaperones, the stores which were beguiling and exciting, but safe, and this was empowering for women. The department store was selling a dream, a fantasy, and was like a drug dealer, peddling an Aladdin's cave of treasures.

Soon after the store moved to Coney Street it also provided employment for many women, who worked long hours for low pay but who found a freedom they had not known before. As time went on Leak and Thorp was a pioneer in large striking window displays and ready-made garments, with clothes for everyone, not just the rich. For it to last nearly a century and a half is testimony to its importance in York. Shopping in York today owes a great deal to its predecessor.

— *Chapter 4* —
FASHION HOUSES

In the 19th and 20th centuries, Coney Street was certainly the fashion centre of the city. The three main and longest lasting fashion houses were Kirby and Nicholson, Grisdale's and Leak and Thorp but there were also plenty of smaller establishments. Since the 18th century there had been an abundance of milliners, mantle and trimming sellers, tailors and woollen drapers in the street, and being a dressmaker or costumier was a respectable occupation for a single lady or a widow such as Madame Catherine Snarry, who had her premises at number 24, and Mrs Eleanor Dillon, who was a corset maker at number 8, succeeded by her daughters Misses Emily and Cecily Dillon in 1889. Some ladies offered an even greater range. Mirabella Metcalfe, parasol manufacturer and seller of lobby cloth, had her shop in Spurriergate, and Martha Marshall, at 6 Coney Stret, sold jewellery, toys and fishing tackle, as well as manufacturing spinning wheels.

But the bigger establishments such as Iles, the dressmaker and ladies tailor, which came to 23 Coney Street at the end of the 19th century and stayed for many years, were usually run by men. At 52 Coney Street, Walton Brothers hosiers and general drapers and milliners advertised in 1897,

Dresses, black crepons, divided skirts, golf jerseys, gloves. We are special agents for the 'watch spring corset'.

Hazell and Miles advert, 1910

In the same year Hazell and Miles had a four storey shop at 20 Coney Street, selling ribbons, hosiery, sunshades, jet ornaments, accessories and trimmings for dressmakers. In 1914 they advertised,

Ladies kid and suede gloves at 1s 11½d.
The Durander original British hose, guaranteed against holes for 3 months, half the price of foreign makes, from 3/1d to 5/9d.

By the 1920s and '30s many of these had disappeared. At number 3 Coney Street, Murfin and Thorpe specialised in corsets (from 1900 to the Second World War) though latterly they branched out to include other types of clothing. Jaeger House opened at number 6 and lasted until the 1980s. Miss Florence Rymer was a costumier at number 15, whilst Mrs Mabel Battrick, Miss Edith Ward and Miss Doris Eshelby sold their wares at 51 Coney Street.

By the 1960s and 1970s fashions were changing dramatically. Richard Shops and Etam in Coney Street, and Chelsea Girl at 9 Spurriergate were the first boutiques in York aimed at young women, selling clothes at a cost affordable to working girls, and Jaeger, Noel Fashions, Bradmore Gowns, Cresta Silk Fashions, Maddox Fashions, Woman's World ladies outfitter, and Wetherall House Fashions all catered for the more traditional look. A new type of shop also opened in the early 1970s, with Ricky Outsize Gowns and Evans Outsize.

JOHN GRISDALE LTD

Exterior of Grisdale's 1900 (James Grisdale)

In September 1900 John Grisdale was only 26 when he rented a small former jeweller's shop in Coney Street. His motto was 'never miss an opportunity'. He had started his career as an apprentice draper in Bowness, followed by a period in Leeds studying fashion, then worked at a draper's shop in Spurriergate, before he opened John Grisdale Ltd. This allowed him to 'enter into a lifelong marital and business partnership' with his wife Jessie. Initially they lived above the shop until they moved into a house in Dringhouses.

The business was very successful and made a profit straightaway. The account book for the first few years includes the following entries:

22 January 1901. Queen Victoria died at 6.30pm. Run on black costumes and jackets. (The shop was closed on February 2nd for the Queen's funeral).
12 June 1901. Big event 10pm (Daughter Doris).
24 June 1902. King indisposed, coronation postponed, great disappointment.
7 October 1902. Son Jack born 11pm.
25 May 1904. Son Norman born.

Interior of Grisdale's 1900 (James Grisdale)

Within a few years of opening, they also had a branch in Darlington and in 1919 they extended into No 23 Coney Street, next door. The shop hours at that time were 8am to 8pm.

The advert for York Shopping Week in 1910, offered

Coats and skirts in the new pastille friezes, all colours from 42s.
Black and navy suits in every fashionable style, from 29/6d to 7 guineas.
Real Harris, Donegal and Scotch tweed, touring and sporting suits. 29/6d to 6 guineas.
Covert coats in raglan, 21s to 5 guineas.
Skirts in black and navy, plain gored, from 10/6d.
Best Scotch tweed, golf and holiday skirts 21s.
Mantles, silk coats, cream sand-cloth coats.

Edith Tavender worked at Grisdale's before the First World War as a cook.

> *I was there four years. I used to cook for the staff, the shop girls, Mr and Mrs Grisdale and the family, about twenty every day. They'd come at twelve o'clock, first sitting, then half of them at one. I used to dress well and have my hair done nice. I used to get some lovely clothes there, at cost. They didn't like you to look slovenly. She wept when I left, she said, "I am sorry you're going, you've never spoilt a thing yet".*

Joan Sadler remembers

> *the very first coat I bought when I started working, was from Grisdale's, 2 guineas. It was a tweed winter coat, a button through one, no belt or anything. You could wear it over every-thing. It was very personal service. They would take you into a dressing place and help you off and on. You wouldn't go into one of those shops unless you intended buying anything. The days of*

big fashion stores, when they got personal service, ended after the war.

In 1919 John Grisdale became the first President of the York Chamber of Trade. Later he was Chairman of the Rotary, and twice the Master of the Merchant Taylor's.

In 1925, his son Norman joined the firm. A year later it became a limited company with directors John, Jessie and Norman Grisdale. In 1931 a new shop front was put in.

In 1939 the company was advertising the 'Grisdale mac in all colours at 21s – guaranteed waterproof for 2 years', and 'Furs altered and repaired by our own expert hands'.

John Grisdale (James Grisdale)

Lady Gillian Barron, Michael Saville and Tina Territt who live in the York area and James Grisdale in Italy are all grandchildren of James and Jessie. Gillian and Michael are children of Doris who was born in 1901 over the shop. Gillian recalls,

Grandpa hunted with the York and Ainsty South. They had a stables at Dringhouses and he had a horse. Granny had a pony and trap. They were very different, he and Granny. She was very stunning. They arrived in August 1900, married at Ledsham just off the A1, and a fort-

night later they opened the business in Coney Street. The clothes never wore out. They weren't ultra fashionable, they were good bread and butter clothes, very well made like Roland Gaunt, abbreviated to Rogaunt. Miss Dales [the First Sales] *would say, "I think I've got something that would suit you".*

It was a big family business. The workshop downstairs was for doing alterations. Very often the hem or the sleeves were too long. There was a member of staff, Miss Umpleby, and she was the only one that could see what length the hem needed to be when you tried on something. "Fetch Miss Umpleby up". They used to wear dark collars. They had to be smart. She had these pins in a pin cushion, back of her hand.

The showroom was on the ground floor, then you went up the staircase in the corner. Granny had this little room halfway up, and a chaise longue in it, and she would lie down. There was a window right onto Coney Street on each side, which would have maybe three dummies with dresses on, displayed quite nicely. Clothes were not actually out on display apart from the windows. Immediately something had been taken off a dummy, it had to be covered over. That was the height of indecency, an uncovered dummy in the window.

I can remember being taken down there when the Duke and Duchess of York came, before they were king and queen. They drove along Coney Street, and we watched them from above. It must have been 1936 or '37.

Granny used to go across to Boots to the library. I had a whole set of the Romany books. When they got the four children, and the business to run, they got a housekeeper who we called Auntie Katie who looked after the house.

Jessie Grisdale with Doris and Jack, c. 1903 (Lady Gillian Barron)

They had about 20 staff, with the cook and half a dozen down in the work room and Harry the porter. He rode a bicycle, like a butcher's bike.

Michael Saville recalls,

Presentation was the key thing. You felt when you went in that you were important. If you wanted to get good clothes you always went to Grisdale's. It was one of the outstanding shops for quality certainly in York, and if you were anybody, you came. It had great drawing power. Being a market town as it was, people would come probably two days a week, when the market place was along Parliament Street.

It had an open entrance, a display just inside. It was long with a series of cubicles, curtained off. The cash desk just on the left and two offices, one for Granny and then the workroom next door.

They used to have the staff lunches, that was an important part. The shop always closed. And the coffee morning at Border's. They always had time to do that. They would all [local shop owners] meet there and discuss the pros and cons of business in the street.

In later years particularly when my grandfather found driving difficult, and I'd just got my driving test, he asked if I would drive him up in his Sunbeam Talbot to the Lake District. I probably learnt more in the four days that I was up there in Windermere, it was good hunting country and he'd take me and show me all these things. He had so much knowledge.

York Drapers' Ball 1957. L to R: Beryl Grisdale, Norman Grisdale, Mrs Shaw, John Grisdale, Jessie Grisdale. (James Grisdale)

Tina Territt is the

daughter of Jessie Grisdale who was the youngest daughter of John and Jessie. But my mother was known as Mary because there was already a Jessie in the family.

If you talk to a lot of the older generation in York, whatever their background, they will tell you, "Oh yes I remember John Grisdale's". There was Granny and Grandpa and then Miss Dale. Mother used to cover when Norman was away, Miss Dales would be next in line. In summer, they all used to go to the Lakes for a month by train, all the family.

They had good quality clothes, a lot of which came from the Leeds warehouses. Certainly the suppliers that I went to with mother looking for stuff, it was good quality clothing, people like Kojama. But fur coats came from London.

Most of the clothing was behind these sliding doors. You didn't go raking through, you said, "I'd like a brown tweed skirt", and they would bring them to you. If there was something slightly more modern as time evolved, they would bring that as well.

Stuff was sent all over the place, it wasn't just local people. If Mrs So-and-So lived up on the moors, as they did do, and they only came in once a month or every two months, her order would be dispatched out in the post.

Val Cason was born in 1942.

When I left school at 15 I went to Grisdale's and worked there for three years. They were a wonderful family to work for. I was Second Sales on separates. It was quite busy and people would sit and wait to be served by the head lady. They did all

Grisdale's shop 1932 after extension and merger of numbers 22 and 23 (James Grisdale)

the alterations themselves downstairs in the workroom. We had five staff on the floor not including Mrs Grisdale. One was a window dresser.

You'd got to be smart. If I literally just scratched my foot, [Mrs Grisdale would say], *"Lift your foot up dear". "Don't cross your hands dear, put your hands down". Yes deportment was the thing.*

Mrs Grisdale would sit on the ottoman in a cubicle, curtained off. She was a lovely lady. We also kept the robes of the Lord Mayor in a cupboard locked up. We'd give them a bit of a shake, and brush the fur.

We had facilities for tea and coffee. We'd sometimes take bread and dripping, we had a fork and would sit toasting on the gas stove.

We had two porters. One did the cellar work, everything had to be wrapped up in tissue paper and in a box with string. If we weren't selling, we had to go and wrap them up. When they wanted things altering, and believe me they had them renewed, Miss Price was the head in the fitting room department, she'd alter the sleeves, the waist, the length, everything practically remade. Must have cost a bomb. And the clothes were expensive.

Grisdale's 1954 *(James Grisdale)*

You spent hours with them, trying different things on. Some of them came for half a day. If they were going to a wedding or the Mansion House, if they were spending £100 it was a lot of money. Some of the stuff was exclusive, very expensive. They'd have a rail full of stock but they'd be different sizes, different colours.

My first wage was £2-7s-6d for the week. Then I gave ten shillings [50p] *for house-keeping.*

In June 1961 a meeting was held at Leak and Thorp concerning the formation of the Coney Street Association, aimed at raising the status of the shopping centre, and working together on issues such as lighting, traffic and parking. The first chairman was Norman Collinson of Leak and Thorp. Ralph Rowntree followed him and in 1963 he was succeeded by Norman Grisdale. There was obviously rivalry between stores but also a spirit of cooperation which was necessary 'to maintain and enhance the dignity and prestige of this famous and historic street'.

In October 1961 Jessie Grisdale died at the age of 87, followed only months later by her husband John in June 1962. Norman remained in charge. In 1963 they were advertising:

For every occasion throughout the year –
ladies' suits, coats, gowns
and furs from

John Grisdale
L T D

39 CONEY STREET · YORK
and 10/11 HIGH ROW · DARLINGTON

Grisdale's advert 1950s

Spring two pieces in plain and patterned Courtelle and Crimplene, around £13-19s-6d, wool jersey three-pieces at £11-19s-6d, inexpensive pure silks, screen printed and fully lined costing a mere 7½ to 8 guineas. A three-quarter ocelot trimmed model at £33-15s, and llama three-quarter coats at 12 guineas for meets and point to points.

When Norman retired, the family business of Grisdale Ltd ceased trading and the premises were sold to W H Smith in 1970, which had moved from its shop further along the street.

SWEARS AND WELLS

Swears and Wells were furriers at 41 Coney Street in the 1950s. The shop later became the Singer Sewing Machine Co.

Sheila Keane worked there in 1952 when,

> *I was 15. I was there till '58 just before I got married. It was next to Woolworth's, and the other side was Grisdale's. There was a seamstress, a manager, a cashier, and three sales persons. I was the third salesperson and it wasn't very often that I got to serve because they worked on commission then. The first saleswoman would rush to get a customer finished then she would take the next one. We had to be in black. Black skirt, white blouse, black cardigan and black shoes.*
>
> *You had to look busy, had to make sure the coats were on hangers properly. Made sure the buttons, the tags were fastened. We'd sometimes help the seamstress if she was turning up. There was a workshop at the back if they wanted any alterations.*

A fur coat was a status symbol, the height of luxury. Famous people like Liz Taylor in the '50s were often seen in mink and ermine, boosting sales enormously. For those with less money the shop sold cheaper coats.

Some of the cheaper coats were very cheap, very poorly made. They used to be put in front of the window to draw people in. Beaver, cony, rabbit. People that wanted a good coat didn't look at those.

We had mink, ermine, musquash. The top class ones were hundreds. We'd try them on in the shop, when we weren't busy, swagger about. There were swing mirrors. I never wanted a fur coat, even though I worked there and tried them on. Mink coats had a flair with them but the majority were just a straight coat, buttoned at the front, hook and eye that you fastened with.

There was an arcade as you went in, a tiled floor, then the show-room, then at the back was the seamstress. Up the stairs was toilets and a kitchen. There was mice running around all over upstairs. There was only a very dim light and one ran over my foot one time. I was scared to death.

The first saleslady, she was a lot older than us, and I got real friendly with her and her sisters, I used to go away for week-ends with them. They had a caravan on the coast. I was paid about 19/11d. I got a rise up to about 30s, that was the most I got.

I remember one time, the models we had in the window, they weren't really very explicit (they had heads and busts I suppose), one lady came in very irate and upset and said, "Please put a coat on the model in the window". It had only been off about five minutes because it was being shown to someone.

All in all it was a quiet place. Now in Coney Street, there's shops blaring out the music before you even go in. They're only for young people really.

KIRBY AND NICHOLSON (LATER ROWNTREE'S)

John and Charles Potter opened a business at 46 Coney Street in 1836, as linen draper, silk mercer, hosier, glover and haberdasher. John Potter died in 1869, Charles retired the following year and the business was sold to their nephew George Potter-Kirby who went into partnership with John Ward Nicholson. The premises by then were at number 2 Coney Street. The adjoining house was purchased and it reopened as Kirby and Nicholson, ladies and children's outfitters, in 1874 and was refurbished in 1878.

NEW AUTUMN FASHIONS
AT
KIRBY & NICHOLSON'S

NEW AND
EXCLUSIVE

GOWNS
COATS
COSTUMES
FUR COATS
MILLINERY
SHOES
—
INSPECTION
CORDIALLY INVITED
—
ESTABLISHED 1847

Telephone 3557.   KIRBY & NICHOLSON (YORK) LTD.,
2, 3 & 4 CONEY STREET, YORK.

George Potter-Kirby was Sheriff in 1901 and elected alderman in 1906. Nicholson died in 1917, and Potter-Kirby in 1924. He left £25,430 in his will, something of a fortune at that time. His son George Arthur became head of the business, and was Master of the Merchant Taylor's for the third time in 1955 in recognition of 50 years of membership. He died in 1967 aged 88 and the business was sold to William Rowntree, originally a draper from Scarborough. When he died in 1901, his son William Stickney Rowntree took over as director, he was the third

Kirby and Nicholson advert

(*Yorkshire Evening Press*)

cousin of Joseph Rowntree the cocoa manufacturer. William died in 1939 and was succeeded by Howard Rowntree and finally Ralph Kenway Rowntree.

The last family link was broken when Ralph retired in 1968. Debenham's made a bid to take over the store in 1965 but the Rowntree name was kept until it changed to Debenham's in November 1972. Major structural alterations to the 'Young Rowntree' department, meant that it was officially reopened as 'Just In', a boutique for women of all ages.

Debenham's continued to flourish and announced in December 1984 that they were to open two Sundays in defiance of the Sunday trading laws. In 1985 they bought the old Marshall and Snelgrove department store in Davygate. The Coney Street store was refurbished in 1987, but merged with the Davygate store in 1990, and closed in 1992. Today Café Rouge is on the site.

Carol Addy worked at Rowntree's,

I'd only be 15, a junior. I fancied working there so I just wandered in and they said, "Would you like to meet our store manager?" They put me on the gown department. You had to be a certain height to work upstairs because the women before us were quite personable young ladies in their 30s, 40s, 50s of quite well-off families. It was seen as the place to work. If you had to model clothes for the customer, you would show them off to the best of your ability. So in the early '60s, there were small girls on the ground floor and taller girls on the second floor.

It was a real hierarchy of buyers and older assistants, who were very much revered, then slightly younger people and then the juniors. You had to be very polite, we were never allowed to go onto the shop floor without being made up. It was a fantastic place to work, I found it very enchanting and very glamorous

Rowntree's 1957 advert (Yorkshire Evening Press)

which you don't seem to get now unless it's Harvey Nicholls. We had an art director, Mr Mason, in charge of the displays, who worked between York and Scarborough. He was terribly glamorous, a bit like Noel Coward. He mesmerised me. He used to float in and say, "I feel blue today". So we'd have blue things all over, all the mannequins would have blue. One day he said, "We need to have this little girl", as he called me, "to model this little suit for the juniors". And I went into the fitting room. When I came out, "Oh a lovely little girl in a lovely little suit". We had a resident model called Marjorie. Penny Hodges from the perfumery department, very pretty with blonde hair in a ponytail, used to model bikinis round the store. Marjorie was wonderful. She looked like Sophia Loren, big almond eyes and very tanned, pitch black hair, a *very middle class lady but such fun. She used to get away with murder because everybody was madly in love with her. She'd say, "I'm going for lunch darling, see you later", and she'd be gone for five hours. She'd come floating back in and we'd think she was going to be in trouble, and she never was.*

She had a dressing room in the gown department. I'd go down and put her hair up in different chignons and French knots. At lunchtimes the buyers would say, "Miss Butterfield, would you do my hair?" And would give me half a crown. I'd use loads and loads of hairspray and fix it with pins. There were three fitting rooms in the gown department and more round the corner. We used to stand them up on a big round drum and if it needed to be altered, the fitters who had a little room of their own up in the attic, one would come down with pins on her arm and pins in her mouth. Everybody was madam. They'd pin the dress up and very carefully put a silk scarf over her head to make sure her make-up didn't go on it. Very often you would dress the lady from top to toe. You'd sell them a suit to go to the races and then you'd say, "Has madam a hat for this? I have the very thing downstairs". It was all personal service. "I've just seen the most beautiful shade of lipstick which would look fabulous with this dress". "What about some wonderful perfume?" Those people would come back time and again because they were so looked after.

Suzy Brown worked in the office at Rowntree's in 1964.

I got my first job as a shorthand typist. I was 16, having left school at 15 and studied at York Technical College. The store also had a furnishings and carpet department in Lendal just up the road, and I'd go there twice a day, to take down letters in shorthand, come back and type them up and return for them to be signed by the head of department. So that was quite a nice thing, to get out and have a wander up the street and back again.

The offices were a hive of activity. There were about four short-hand typists working for the Director, the Secretary, the buyers and the heads of departments. There were a couple of girls on adding machines and the window dressers had a room. It was just like 'Are you Being Served?' The buyers were very much king of the castle. We all wore the same overalls. I remember one style being turquoise striped with long sleeves and a zip up the front made from nylon. It was awful.

Suzy Grey 1968 (Suzy Brown née Grey)

Mr Mason, who was very flamboyant, would waltz in one day a week, arms flying about, shouting for someone to help him type up the programme for the following week. He spoke so quickly and he wanted it doing straightaway on the typewriter. Usually the Director's secretary would do it and we would breathe a sigh of relief, but she left and then I took it on. I was nervous at first, but the others were relieved not to do it.

We worked on Saturdays and had Sunday and Mondays off. Saturdays in Coney Street were very busy. My wages in 1964 were £3-16s-6d a week. Sometimes I would relieve the switchboard operator whilst she went for lunch and it was the old fashioned type of rods being pushed into the relevant hole to connect to the caller.

There would be at least 20 departments, haberdashery, dresses, coats, umbrellas, handbags, underwear, and perfume. There was a canteen downstairs. I never had breakfast, I always waited, and as soon as it opened up, I'd go down as my first break and have a roll and a cup of tea.

You did feel a little bit more important working upstairs in the office because you were in touch with the director of the store and the buyers. We were a happy bunch and we socialised out of hours as well.

Jean Rudka (née Handley) started at Rowntree's in 1947 at the age of 15 and

learnt tailoring, alterations to clothes sold in the shop. When I first started I hadn't a clue. I didn't even know basting cotton from ordinary cotton. I remember them stressing, always get a shade darker cotton to blend in with what you're sewing. People bought clothes, were fitted and measured, and we altered them. I had to learn all that. I did get as far as learning to do the dressmaking. But like in every trade it all altered.

The workshops were upstairs. It was a very elite shop, one of the best dress shops in York. You went down the side and up the back stairs which were terrible. Upstairs in the workshop

97

it was very bare, no carpets. The two tailors, the gentlemen, were in one room. They did ladies skirts and things. As you got further advanced and you were making a skirt, you did it with basting double, then where it was going to be pleated you lifted it up and cut it through. I'm afraid in my younger days I cut it out wrong. So the lady, instead of getting pleats in a certain place, she got them in a different place. I think there were five or six [in our room], at low tables. Miss Taylor, the lady over us all, always sat on the end.

We did a lot by hand but there were machines. I think we all seemed to do something different. When you're first learning you've got the easy jobs but probably the horrible jobs as well.

The manageress, Miss Smith, she was over all the shop, but we were not supposed to eat in the workshop. You know what it's like, we usually took something. We could never understand, she always seemed to come breezing in. It was ever so many years after that we found out, straight across,

Jean Handley and Ada Thomas 1949 (Jean Rudka née Handley)

above Burgin's on the corner, it was a hairdresser and her sister worked there and she'd ring her and say, "They're eating!".

There was a gentleman, he'd obviously been in the war and he'd come to the Mansion House every morning at a regular time, dressed in a top hat and black. And I think it was like shell shock. He came and stood and saluted.

But it was not all work.

When people came to the Mansion House, the Queen Mother came, we'd hang out over the window, they did allow us just to see them come and go. We used to take a packed lunch and we'd climb to the top of the Minster, eat our lunch and then go back to work. We went on trips, on a coach, to places like the Lakes

Jean Handley seated bottom right with work colleagues (Jean Rudka née Handley)

and Aysgarth Falls, probably twice a year. Ada and I, she was older than me, we got on well and used to go to the pictures on a Saturday night. We were all happy there, there was never any falling out.

Jean also had a friend who

worked in Anderson's and she was dark and I mean in those days there wasn't many black people about. I had to go to Anderson's and she did tailoring there. We became really good friends. She didn't have a good time of it. People could be very nasty to her. She was a lovely lady, from Malaya I think.

Janet Pigott recalls a fashion shop in the 1950s,

Half way up Coney Street, called Vogue. It sold beautiful evening dresses as well as smart day wear. One day I went in and asked the price of an evening dress in shot taffeta. From one angle it looked a very dark navy-blue or black, but from another angle it looked green. It was absolutely stunning, but so was the price. I couldn't afford it and I had to walk out without it. It was a phenomenal sum of money compared with what I got paid.

By the 1960s work was plentiful in the retail trade, and many girls leaving school aspired to work in a fashion shop, though it was not as glamorous as it seemed.

VAN ALLAN

Catherine Suter started work in 1961 at Van Allan at 34 Coney Street. She recalls,

It was a ladies' dress shop and it sold only dresses and coats. I

joined when I was 15 and anything under 18, you were a junior. If someone came into the shop, a senior person would walk forward, greet them and ask them if they could be of any help. If I got to serve a customer, I'd basically look at their body and figure out what size they were. We'd go into the fitting rooms with them. We had to help them dress and undress, which I know I myself wouldn't have liked but that's the way it had to be. We were on commission, three old pence out of every pound which wasn't a lot. I was getting £3-2s a week.

Catherine Suter, 1960s
(Catherine Suter)

We had to wear black, I had to buy my own black dress before I went. If we did want to buy anything, we'd get ten per cent off. Most of it was not my style. It was geared more towards the older lady. I did buy a couple of dresses, one was a cotton summer dress. I used to go to the Court School of Dancing.

I was into dresses with big skirts so I could wear petticoats underneath.

We had a male manager, Mr Poole. He was very nice, bit of a joker. I was very naïve. As the junior I had to run errands and he'd tell me to go to Crow's Butchers in Spurriergate to get him a warm pork pie and sausage roll.

He sent me once for a ham sandwich, stipulating no mustard. I brought it back and it had mustard on and he told me I had to take it back. I was devastated but I did take it back and I came back with a sandwich without the mustard and he just about fell through the floor. He said he couldn't believe it, and he was only joking.

One lunchtime I'd gone to get my ears pierced and when I came back, Mr Poole told me that pierced ears were not allowed in the shop. I just didn't know what to do. I couldn't take them out. I thought I was going to lose my job. It was Mr Poole and his jokes at work again.

My mother used to work at the Picture House, a part time usherette. My dad, Ernest Bean, worked at Border's, he was a master grocer. I remember when he came home, his hands smelled of bacon. I'd seen him patting the butter into shape.

A friend of mine got an apprenticeship at Maison Lee in Coney Street. Every Tuesday evening I went there for her to practise different hairstyles on me. I used to get my hair done free, never knew what it was going to turn out like. Maison Lee had a hairspray that they always used, their own specific brand. I loved the smell of it. If you passed somebody in the street, you knew that's where they had been because you could smell the hairspray.

In the 1960s everything was on the brink of change, and fashion would never be the same again. Girls no longer wore what their mothers did, they were keen on fashion, inspired by magazines and pop music shows, and wanted to explore their own ideas and designs.

Catherine Suter (on the right) and friends, 1960s (Catherine Suter)

I was interested in clothes, I would keep up with the fashions. I remember Dorothy Perkins and Etam. You could see everything was changing, with mini skirts and then hot pants.

Catherine Pickard remembers,

the Chelsea Girl boutique. It was a really dark shop and it was the in place to go if you were a teenage girl. That always looked like a dark cavern, like something off Carnaby Street. I didn't like the big communal changing room. I preferred Etam because it was brightly lit, and it had nice changing rooms. I got a nice midi skirt and a skinny rib jumper, those were the sort of things you'd wear in the '70s.

Shopping today is a totally different business from the days when Grisdale, Leak and Thorp, and Kirby and Nicholson dominated the centre of York. Today Coney Street still has its fashion shops but they are no longer family firms. Accessorize/Monsoon, Top Shop, Mango, Next, River Island, Wallis, Warehouse, Principles (part of Debenham's) and Dorothy Perkins (with Burton's), are now all international chain stores. Coney Street's oldest clothes shop is British Home Stores which has a franchise to operate stores in 14 other countries. Customers are now allowed to browse without an obligation to buy. Some stores provide catalogues and all encourage buying online. The fashion stores in Coney Street could be almost anywhere in the world.

River Island and Next, on the former site of Leak and Thorp, 2013 (Christine Kyriacou)

— *Chapter 5* —
TAILORS

As well as being the centre of ladies' fashions, Coney Street was also the home of a number of specialised tailors. In 1889 Charles Olley worked as a tailor at number 29, who was replaced by James Maxwell at the beginning of the 20th century. Christopher Annakin Milward was a hosier, glover, hatter and shirt maker at number 14 Coney Street up to the 1920s, after which the building became Stead and Simpson's shoe shop. At number 20–21 was the rather downmarket Fifty Shilling Tailors (below the Willow Café). Later on there were Greenwood's at 17 Spurriergate and Royce Manshops at 8–10 Spurriergate.

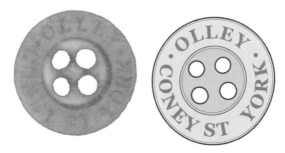

Button from Charles Olley tailor (York Archaeological Trust)

DIXON'S

Tom Dixon's outfitters was based at 53 Coney Street from the 1920s right through to the 1980s.

James Barker recalls going there.

I used their establishment quite a bit. There was certainly personal service. People would wear jackets and ties and look tidy. Now everybody walks about in what I call semi-scruff order, casual clothing just about.

You'd have an idea what you were going for, they were always very attentive. Mr Dixon was there, you had faith in the people you were dealing with. They wouldn't try and fob you off with anything that you didn't feel was suitable for you. Shopping was much more pleasurable in those days.

BURTON'S MENSWEAR

Montague Burton came to England from Lithuania in 1900, and opened his first shop in Chesterfield at the age of 18. By 1929 he had 400 shops, with factories and mills. After the Second World War, his suit for veterans was named 'the Full Monty'. Montague's son Raymond took over the businesses and was also a philanthropist, who contributed to York University and helped to fund many local history projects in York and elsewhere. He died in 2011.

The York branch of Burton's was officially opened by the Lord Mayor at 27 Coney Street in April 1931. (It was later renumbered 52). It also had premises in Ousegate which were extended in 1934. It closed for refurbishment in 1979, and Malcolm McManahan recalls,

The reopening took place on Friday 24th August. The chap who compered it was called Adrian John, York Hospital Broad-casting Service, who I actually did some work with back then. Someone called Fiona Richmond was doing signed photographs at the time. I was on my lunch break from work and I had to go into Coney Street for some reason. This crowd was in the way.

The crowd was there to see celebrity Fiona Richmond and the store held a competition,

They asked the audience and you put your hand up if you knew the answer and I was the only one. So I won a tee shirt and a baseball cap. One of my more productive lunch breaks. I'd be 17.

Malcolm also got a signed photo of Fiona. She was a glamour model and actress, and the girlfriend of Paul Raymond, who opened the country's first strip club and was known as the King of Soho. Just before appearing at Burton's, she had been voted 'Bottom of the Year'!

Burton's tailors, 1950s (Yorkshire Evening Press)

Burton's acquired other businesses including Dorothy Perkins, and the two together now share a store at 29 Coney Street.

ANDERSON'S

Button from Anderson's (York Archaeological Trust)

Anderson's has been called the 'crème de la crème' of British tailoring, and was always described as a high class tailoring, military and clerical outfitters. Robert William Anderson came to York in 1827 as foreman to Richard Evers, a draper at 19 Coney Street. They later went into partnership but this was dissolved and Anderson set up his own business in 1863. He was governor of the Merchant Taylor's three times, before he died in 1887 at the age of 84, and was succeeded by his youngest son, also Robert. In 1907 the business incorporated William Robinson & Sons of St Helen's Square which was founded in 1763. Robert II died in 1906, having been a councillor for the Guildhall ward for a number of years. His son Robert III took over, and he died in January 1953 aged 85, after 70 years service in the business.

His brother, Captain Arthur Anderson, also had a business in Coney Street, as a stationer and bookseller at number 44. During the First World War he was commandant of the York Voluntary Aid Detachment and St John's Ambulance Brigade. He died in 1927. His son Robert Walter was the last of the family. He served in the RAF in the First World War and died in 1967.

Arthur Anderson's Stationer's shop (York Directory)

Anderson's tailoring business was very successful and the balance, for the year ending 28 February 1895, was £2119-0s-6d. £727-10s-1d was still owing from customers. The year's profit was £351-8s-2d but they had to write off £2-17s-3d in bad debts.

An advertisement in 1900 offered,

'Liveries and chauffeurs' uniforms.
Officers' uniforms, accoutrements and helmets', (for which there were testimonials from Lord Wenlock, Colonel of the East Riding Imperial Yeomanry, and Lt Colonel Harrison of the Yorkshire regiment).

The firm was registered by the War Office as 'quality makers of military outfits'.

R. W. ANDERSON & SONS

Tailors Hatters, Hosiers and
===== Shirtmakers, =====

Sole Agents for Burberry Weatherproofs.
Jaeger and Cellular
—— *Clothing.* ——

33, Coney Street, YORK.

Adjoining Black Swan Hotel.   Tailoring Department Opposite.

Telephone No. 0243.

Anderson's advert 1911

By 1903 a catalogue for Anderson's stated that it was now, 'Under Royal patronage'. Tailoring was the speciality at number 15, with ready to wear clothing and hosiery at number 33, and shirt-making and tailoring at St Helen's Square. Other advertisements describe it as 'sporting tailors and outfitters, riding habits, breeches and legging makers, hats, hosiery and shirt making'.

In 1946, the new Governor of Singapore, Sir Franklin Gimson, had his new state uniform tailored in York by Messrs R W Anderson. Sir Franklin said, 'Not for more than a hundred years have they produced a uniform on such resplendent lines'. The cocked hat was made of black silk, with a flat silver tassel with seven silver and eleven crimson bullions. The plume was composed of white swan feathers, measuring ten inches in length with red feathers under them. A double-breasted tailored coat was made of blue cloth, with collar and cuffs of scarlet material with skirts edged in white, and trimmed with silver embroidery. On the silver epaulettes was gold embroidery setting out rose, thistle and shamrock with the crown above. The trousers had silver lace stripes. The sword, which had an ivory grip with long scimitar blade, was also obtained through Anderson's.

Anderson's outfit for the Governor of Singapore

(Anderson Archives)

Patsie Hirstwood started her apprenticeship at Anderson's aged 14, in 1940. She travelled in from Pickering, and was employed in the jacket and coat workroom at 15 Coney Street.

It was something I'd always wanted to do. I had grown up with sewing and good quality fabrics. I just took it for granted. I know we only worked for what were obviously wealthy people. It was the northern equivalent of Saville Row.

I remember going in and talking to Mr Frayn, the head cutter and fitter, and being absolutely fascinated by all the different heavy gauge brown paper pattrons [template]. *They were hung up with string with the customer's name on, and each person's pattron was individual to them. The other cutter and fitter, his were hung in a different place. On the wall was a little box with a voice box and a handle. We couldn't ring out but we could ring upstairs to the shop and they used to ring down.*

Kendall's umbrella store was next door and then there was this passage that went between the two shops. At the end a little landing went round and then down, and an iron staircase went down to basement depth. And that was the height of the garden. There was the cottage where Mr Robert and his wife lived. [This was Robert Walter Anderson, the last of the family]. *Then there were steps up to our workroom. At the bottom left hand side was the door into the kitchen. You came back and up about three steps into the little skirt room. At the other side of the steps and beneath our workroom was another little workroom which females didn't go into. It was the old men's room. Mr Kelly and Mr Smith and a lad older than me, Jacky Hunt, worked in there. Behind the actual shop was what had been a most beautiful garden, but a big air raid shelter had been buried and there was a green mound where it had been turfed over. Then there was the ground floor with the shop. Above that, where Mr Frayn's room was, was a spiral staircase up to the first floor where they had a wooden donkey which was used for fitting ladies with trousers, breeches, jodhpurs, riding apparel.*

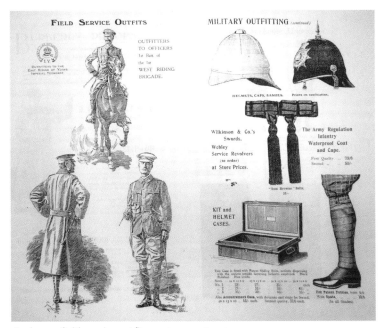

Anderson field service outfits *(Anderson Archives)*

In our workroom it was great coats, jackets, British warms [military coats made from a thick woollen fabric], *a demon to hand stitch due to the thickness but wonderfully warm. At times we worked on trews, breeches and jodhpurs. You worked on different garments at the same time. That's part of any textiles. But first of all you'd get it rolled up as a bundle and tied with tape and that would come to be basted (tacked). Tailors' sewing needles are only very short, tailors' thimbles have no end, you use the back of your finger to the needle. And it would go up and the customer would come in for the first fitting. Some would have two fittings, some would have even more. It would always be the same tailor and the same girl who worked on it. If there was a rush job on, one might say, "Can so-and-so come and help me?" But that is just a high class textile work-room atmosphere. They had fabric sample books. My favourites were Monrospuns.*

There were three sewing machines. There was one ordinary Singer straight stitch machine used only for rush job trouser leg seams or pocket linings, a Dearborn padding machine, used when there was not enough time to do lapel padding by hand, and a basting machine, used only when time did not permit it being done by hand.

I was with Johannes Hoffman, Johnny Hoffman, we had an enormous table, he was the foreman. I sat there, with Freda Milner, Olive Johnson, Jack Douglas.

There were three tables. At the wall backing onto the kitchen and the skirt room was a huge very heavy table and that was where we used to do the shrinking of trews.

Trews are shaped to the leg. They'd got a curve to accommo-date the bent knee. And the inside is the opposite, so you have to shrink the inside, with a damp cloth and a goose, which is a tailor's iron. You just gradually work it out. Trews were used by a lot of regiments, highland regiments and KRRs [King's Royal Rifles]. *We did fine detail. Eyelet hose on belts. Linings for jackets were of Silesia, known as Italian cloth.*

Mr Willie Anderson [Robert William], *he was still there when I left. He was a lovely old man. He sat in the office and super-vised.*

We certainly had a lot of who we referred to as 'the county'. We worked for governor generals' wives. That was when I fell in love with Monrospun. They used to do some very light tropical tweeds. We did do a lot of sporting clothes. There were some jockeys who were very famous and quite wealthy, they always had their racing breeches made when they came to the York meeting. One time I remember us having a box of oranges, it was either an owner or a trainer who brought them in. A great luxury.

We used to go to the tobacconist next door to number 33 [Boulton at number 34] *and they'd let the men have cigarettes from under the counter and one of us girls had to go and get them. They'd go mad if we went back with some called Camel. "What have you brought that rubbish for?" "Well that's all they'd got".*

We had a drink mid morning and mid afternoon. You know they had national milk for babies, there was some sort of drinking chocolate, it was only meant to be apprentices that had it. We just used to all share.

One perk the apprentices had was being able to make their own clothes.

Peter Bond at the corner of Feasegate and Market Street, I would go there and buy fabric. Coats and skirts and costumes. But we only worked on them in our dinner hour. They would cut and fit them for us. So to all intents and purposes we were clothed in Anderson tailored apparel. It was all part of your training.

By the 1960s, the firm was moving into a new era, though still supplying well-known names in tailoring, such as Burberry raincoats, Van Heusen shirts, Maenson and Dack suits, and Cox Moore sweaters.

Jim Boyes, one of the directors, stated that Anderson's was 'built up on the quality of its merchandise' and an article in the York and County Times 1963 read, 'this is a firm where personal service is something more than a slick phrase. They have a history of catering for hunts etc. which goes back some 200 years. You can obtain ready to wear riding clothes or, in four to six weeks, have them made to measure'.

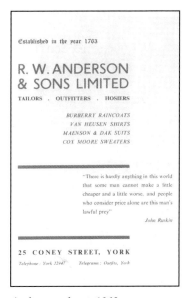

The firm was forced by death duties to sell the Coney Street shop to a chain store, and move to Blake Street in 1969. Jim Boyes was the longest serving member of Anderson's, and after spending 75

Anderson advert, 1963 (James Grisdale)

years there, he received a telegram from the Queen Mother in October 2001. He died in January 2007.

When the business finally closed in 2008, it was the end of two and a half centuries of an internationally known high class tailoring company in York. The ornate door of the Coney Street shop, which had moved to Blake Street, finally went to the Castle Museum.

Jim Boyes (James Grisdale)

— *Chapter 6* —
ENTERTAINMENT *and* LEISURE

In Coney Street in the 18th century, the Mansion House held its own private banquets and musical evenings, and the Assembly Rooms, just round the corner in Blake Street, was the scene of many balls. Coffee houses were very popular and in December 1728 the Yorkshire Herald advertised, 'The Great room of Mr Ward's Coffee House on the corner of Spurriergate, was the setting for the new art of dexterity of hand and the Royal Sword Dance'. Crow's Coffee House, also known as the White Horse, opened in Judges' Lodgings in 1810 but by 1814 it was advertised to let.

For the working classes, organised entertainment is a modern concept. Pubs and private clubs existed, but it was not until the late 19th century that working men's clubs, adult schools, dance halls and community venues made an appearance.

There was plenty of sport all over the city of York, and the river behind Coney Street was used for skating at the times when it was frozen over, and for boating in the summer. Young people with little spending money could spend their time going for walks or listening to bands. In Coney Street there were several pubs, though the two coaching inns were used primarily as staging posts for those travelling elsewhere. At the beginning of the 20th century, there was much more entertainment on offer, as music hall and classical concerts took hold in the city. Cinemas soon came along, often combined with cafés and restaurants, which provided their own orchestras.

THE MONKEY RUN

One way to meet other young people was to parade up and down, usually on Sundays or in the evening, and this was known as the Monkey Run. Coney Street was one area in York where this took place. Young men and women dressed in their finery and walked up and down the street, hoping to meet the opposite sex. One lady recalled how she and her friend would enjoy a walk there, *'laughing and giggling and watching out for lads, though we pretended not to notice them'*. When a young man kept treading on her heels, she soon got annoyed and smacked him on the head. They were married for nearly 50 years.

Not everyone approved of the Monkey Run. As early as 1822, complaints were made about the 'disorderly conduct' of young people in Spurriergate. Five householders in Coney Street 'procured the authority to act as special constables' to try to stop rowdyism in the street. The Lord Mayor called a meeting of parish constables in 1828 to urge greater vigilance after dark.

In March 1900 the Yorkshire Evening Press reported, *'The York police are using every effort to put a stop to the nuisance caused every Sunday night in Coney Street and Spurriergate by young people of both sexes obstructing the footpaths by standing about in groups. At the police court today several young men and women were fined one shilling for this offence. Three boys were fined two shillings for riotous conduct in Coney Street on Saturday night. They were indulging in rough horseplay and pushing girls about'*.

In 1916 the Yorkshire Herald printed a letter from 'A Disabled Belgian Soldier' who complained that, *'In Coney Street about 7pm, there is a rush of young fellows looking to find a girl. If they were on the front, they should not have so much trouble to find a German. If the fellows in the motor-car on Monday or those walking every night in Coney Street to find a sweetheart have a little bit of patriotism, they should enlist at once'*.

After the First World War, the Monkey Run continued. But the Press reported *'a number of cases before the courts concerning young people parading in Coney Street causing obstruction on the footpaths'*. It was suggested that this was *'a case for the social agencies, as these were people all dressed up with nowhere to go'*.

George Kendrew remembers how he and his brothers in the 1930s would

> *walk up and down on a Sunday afternoon, all smartly dressed. You met girls and had a talk. Coney Street was full of young people. There'd be a couple of policemen, they kept you moving, that's all. There was no rowdiness. We all wore straw hats, straw bangers we called them. I remember my mother taking us to a tailor and she bought us three black cloth coats, one each.*

By the 1950s, the Monkey Run was not so appealing, when young people now owned motorbikes and cars. Chris Dowell

> *can remember driving down Coney Street in our old car, the Sunbeam Talbot. The door wouldn't open and the windows wouldn't wind down. We were laughing and joking, a load of lasses. We couldn't wind the window down, and a policeman approached us because he could see we were laughing and giggling. We said, "We've just lost our way, officer".*

> *Coney Street was very quiet then, it had shifted onto the Empire* [now the Grand Opera House] *and round there.*

EBOR HALL

In the 1860s, the Ebor Rooms, behind the Yorkshire Evening Press offices at 10a Coney Street, were advertised as 'Billiard and News Rooms'. In 1881, the place became the York Conservative Club but a few years later, it was known as Ebor Hall. In March 1913, the place held a St Patrick's Day celebration, for the York branch of the United Irish League, offering 'Tea, Irish songs and dances. God save Ireland'. (A contrast from the Conservative Club!)

Ebor Hall on right (Ann Gordon)

For those with spending money, dances were another way of finding partners. During the First World War, these were often populated by soldiers home on leave. In August 1915, dances from 7.30pm to 11.30pm at Ebor Hall cost ninepence, but only sixpence for soldiers. But a ticket for the Boxing Night dance from 8pm to 2am was one shilling. The Hall was advertised as 'to let for private dances, parties, receptions, dinners, teas, meetings. Catering indoors and out. China, glass, silver, tea urns on hire'.

The hall was also opened as a social centre for mothers and wives of soldiers and sailors. Dances continued after the war and in 1919, the Tramways employees held a whist drive and dance offering 'a splendid dance programme' and a Grand Confetti Carnival was advertised with the Corona Orchestra from Scarborough.

In March 1924, the Ebor Hall was the scene of the 'last night of J W Pritchard's Streamer Dances' from 7.30 to 11.30 at a cost of one and sixpence, where streamers of coloured crepe paper were thrown over couples as they danced. JW Pritchard, or Billy as he was known, ran the Blue Chevrons. His sister Violet Taylor who lived at the Leeds Arms on Peasholme Green loved going to the dances.

> *When Billy came back from the war, he decided to get a concert party up. He played the piano. At ten o'clock* [after helping in the pub] *I'd run like mad up Spen Lane and Coney Street to have an hour's dancing at the Ebor Hall. You went down the side of Leak and Thorp and it was beautiful.*

By the 1960s Ebor Hall was used by the Yorkshire Evening Press, partly for storage and partly as a social club. John Avison recalls it being used

> *By our advertising dept. I would go to deliver advertising copy. I remember it as a distinctive, I suppose you could say Spanish brickwork, light coloured bricks round the arches.*

THE FLYING SERVICES CLUB

Ebor Hall had disappeared before the Second World War but the Flying Services Club, at 33 Coney Street, held dances and concerts, including, on 21st October 1948, a 'Grand Concert with Jack Keeler and his piano and other artistes'. Jazz sessions were also held at the club during this period, with the music of the Night Flyers.

The Flying Services Club is not mentioned after 1948, but the York-shire Evening Press advertised a concert at the Gunners Club in Coney Street in February 1949, and this may well have been the same place. In 1953 the Artillery Club in Coney Street held jazz sessions and whist drives. By the 1960s there is no more mention of these clubs.

David Wilson, whose father was the caretaker at the Guildhall recalls joining the

> *Gunners' Club, a music club with bands playing. When Ted Heath came to York, we were there and Jack Parnell and his quartet came up and played. My friend Keith Laycock* [a well-known York double bass player] *used to play up there.*

THE BLACK SWAN

The earliest mention of the Black Swan coaching inn, which was on the site of the present British Home Stores, was in 1663. It was said to be one of the oldest coaching inns in the country. In the 1820s over 130 horses were stabled there. Daily mail and passenger coaches departed from the inn, including the 'Express' to Carlisle two mornings a week, the 'Rockingham' going to Hull every morning, and the 'Trafalgar' to Hull every afternoon. The 'Union' went to Kendal every morning, and the 'True Blue' to Leeds each afternoon. Other coaches left for Liverpool, Scarborough, Sheffield and even London. A handbill of 1706 offered, *'A Stage Coach from the Black Swan in Coney Street to the Black Swan in Holborn, London, every Monday, Wednesday and Friday, which performs the journey in four days if God permits. It sets forth at five in the morning, allowing each Passenger 14lb weight and all above 3d a pound'.*

In 1840 there were 20 coaches a day but by 1842 mail coaching was coming to an end. The advent of the railways had revolutionised transport. By 1902 there was only accommodation for 30 men and stabling for 30 horses though it was still used by travellers.

Bill from Black Swan (*York Explore Local History Archives*)

The inn closed on 4 April 1939 and was demolished in 1968. A number of people remember an amusement arcade on the site during the Second World War. Brian Wilson recalls,

It was in the yard of the Black Swan. You went from Coney Street down a concrete lane beside the pub, into this arcade. It was not well lit, but it had a roof on, and it had slot machines, where you put a penny in, and sometimes would get twopence

back. It was like Gala Land in Scarborough. It was privately owned. I was eight in 1939 when the war started and I remember going there. We were allowed to roam about in those days. I imagine somebody thought that it was a good way of making money.

It does not appear in any street directories as it was probably there for the duration of the war, and was a form of entertainment often used by soldiers.

THE GEORGE INN

Originally the George and the Dragon and then the Golden Lion, the George Inn was mentioned in 1603.

According to the Yorkshire Herald, it had also been known as The Bull, then during Henry VIII's reign it became the Rose. In 1459 it was decreed that 'no aliens from foreign parts shall be lodged within the city or suburbs, but only in the Inn at the sign of The Bull in Conyng Street'.

The George Inn
(Ian Collinson)

124

In 1736 it was described as one of three principal inns in the city. In 1622 John Taylor, the 'Water Poet', sailed from London to York in an open boat. He offered to sell the boat to the Lord Mayor, who refused, and the boat was bought by the landlord of the George, Thomas Kaye. Taylor then wrote,

I sold the boat, as I supposed most meet,
To honest Mr Kaye in Cunny Street,
He entertained me well, for which I thank him,
And gratefully amongst my friends I'll rank him.

The sisters Charlotte and Anne Brontë stayed there in 1849 on the way to Scarborough, where Anne subsequently died, but less than 20 years later the inn was sold by auction in May 1866 in five lots which became shops.

In 1869 Leak and Thorp bought part of the site, with Thomas Horsley, gun merchants, in the other part. The Royal Room, used for the accommodation of royalty, was divided into two. The stained glass window was taken out and sold in London. The wine cellar was let to the Conservative Club.

THE HELMET

This inn is mentioned in 1660, when the innholder Christopher Browne was taken to court for 'allowing a fence to lie down', causing damage to the value of 20s. There is no mention after 1673.

THE LEOPARD

The *Leopard* was situated in Leopard Yard, between numbers 47 and 48 Coney Street. William Petch was landlord in 1778 and it was for sale in 1826 and again to let in 1854. It closed in 1907 when its licence expired

and was demolished in November 1924.
THE GOLDEN CUP and CROWN AND PEARL

In the 1700s, a watchmaker called Boverick lived in Low Ousegate but took orders for work at the Golden Cup, Coney Street. Another craftsman, who made ivory ships completely rigged and fitted with brass guns, and crafted embroideries with human hair, operated from the Crown and Pearl.

THE GREYHOUND

The Greyhound, situated next to Woolworth's, was first mentioned in the York Courant of July 1772. It was sold by auction in November 1838. John Linfoot, the landlord, had been charged with assault on his wife in December 1836. There were many changes of ownership during the ensuing years.

In 1876 George Exelby was dismissed from the pub on an assault charge, and his son Harry became landlord but died at the age of 34 in 1891. There were three more landlords before George Douglass became licensee in 1935. He was there for 21 years until November 1956. The last landlord was Harold Dalton and after his death in 1957, numbers 10–16 Coney Street were sold by auction. Waterloo Place, a row of houses behind the pub and the river, had already been demolished.

George Douglass's son Brian recalls

I was born at Milsom Grove. Father was an insurance rep, then he got the pub at Tadcaster. We moved to York to the Greyhound to take care of my father's mother, the year my grandfather died, about 1936.

It went up four storeys. When you went in, off to your left was a smoke room. Through the other door, it was a long narrow pub, in fact they built us a fire escape over onto Woolworth's roof because there was no way out if we got a hit during the war. There was the brewery company dead opposite Woolworth's, and then a solid wall, so it was just a tunnel. At the end was ladies' toilets and then the stairs carried on up to our living quarters, and the gents' toilets and the cellars went off on the other side. So all the fumes and everything came in, you had to keep the

Greyhound Hotel (Brian Douglass)

window shut all the time. It was rough.

During the war it was a soldiers' pub. Beer you couldn't get, spirits you could. My dad used to take my mother on a motor-bike through to Leeds and they'd come back with this sack in between her and him. My mother ran it during the war when father joined the National Fire Service, then went into the RAF. They went to court and transferred the licence into her name. She was a strong woman. One night, a soldier insulted her and he was taken outside and never came in again. Three lads carried him out. They looked after her, the regulars. She used to make what they called a Spitfire cocktail which was almost non-alcoholic but it sold like wildfire. But there was a lot of ladies of the night. They'd be asking for expensive drinks, but my mother used to swing 'em these cheap ones so the soldiers wouldn't be out of pocket.

At night the pianist would always end with 'Deep Purple'. I'd sit upstairs, my little sister died and I was on my own then, and listen for 'Deep Purple'. I knew it was closing time and I'd creep down and help to cash up, add the pennies up.

THE PICTURE HOUSE

The Picture House cinema (which seated 1000) and restaurant opened on 12 April 1915, with the film 'When East meets West', at number 2 Spurriergate, at a cost of £10,000. The site had previously been occupied by Hamilton and Hall, grocers. The latest bioscope machines were used to show films. Entertainment was important during the First World War and films were shown continuously every day but Sunday from 2.30 to 10.30pm, and the café

Picture House early days (York Oral History Society)

was open from 10am to 10pm, with the orchestra playing from 3.30 to 5.30pm and 7.30 to 10pm.

The cinema ran an uninterrupted service for the next forty years, apart from in 1947 when the front stalls were under several feet of flood water. In 1920 the Picture House Orchestra under the direction of

Alfred Wilde regularly played a selection of classical and jazz music. Most cinemas across the country had either organs or orchestras at this time, and Alfred Wilde's 'Famous York Quintette' described itself as 'one of the finest picture house quintettes in the country'.

Picture House bill

Picture House advert, 1915

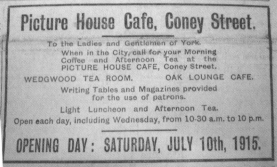

As well as the popular films of the time, in September 1921 the cinema showed a Public Health film 'The End of the Road', a seven-part film authorised by the National Council for Combating Venereal Diseases. Children under 14 were not admitted.

In 1929, the owners, Provincial Cinema Theatres, were taken over by Gaumont and in 1930 the cinema was busy with the installation of the talkies. Although the first talkie, or film with sound, appeared in America in October 1927, it took a year for it to premier in London, and another few years for sound to become a global phenomenon.

The York directory for 1929–30 advertises the Picture House Café as York's premier and most central,

'For morning coffee, four course lunch at 2s, dainty afternoon teas, and grills served at shortest notice. Private parties catered for'. For 2s 6d, a lunch of steak and kidney pie, with cabbage, mashed potato and rice pudding was on offer.

Moyra Johnson was born in 1915 and was one of the country's first

Moyra Johnson and glider, 1930s (Moyra Johnson)

women glider pilots.

I had a boyfriend called Philip and he took me to the Picture House in his car. He went away to park it and left me in the entrance talking to the cinema manager who was Ernest Johnson. I happened to tell him I was going to the Banker's Ball with Philip the next day, so I went to the ball and Ernest was there. Philip got drunk so Ernest took me home. We were married within the year. We got a flat in East Mount Road, and we bought all the stuff for it from Woolworth's, because it was next door to the Picture House and Ernest knew the manager there. So we got everything for the kitchen and all the little bits and pieces. But we never actually moved in. A fortnight before we were married he was moved to a cinema in South Shields. The war broke out a year later, and Ernest decided to volunteer for the RAF.

Moyra Johnson being interviewed by the author (Mike Race)

Ernest was born in Goole in 1910.

I was assistant manager at the Majestic at Leeds, and then there was a racket on at the Picture House in York, where they were fiddling the tickets. There was a pageboy in league with one of the checkers in the stalls. They'd have half the tickets, but the checker had some old tickets in her hand. She palmed the old tickets, handed them to the pageboy who took them up to the cashier, who then sold them again. And we found this was happening and they all got the sack. And so that was my first introduction into queer dealings in cinemas.

I once had to relieve at the Pavilion in Middlesbrough and the cinema was opposite the iron and steel works. There were no women except two lady cashiers, all the rest of the staff were men. The foreman had a big stick and he used to walk up and down the gangway and if anybody started being funny or laughing, he used to lean over and tap them on the head.

Four months after that, my supervisor asked me if I'd like to take the manager's job at the Picture House in Coney Street which I did in 1936.

It was a cinema cum restaurant. There was quite a big foyer, with the most marvellous fireplace on the right hand side, which we used to light with coke in the winter. I'd stand in front of that fire all the time. There was a lift, upstairs was the circle,

VISIT THE   (Tel. 2493.

Picture House Cafe,
(York's Premier and Most Central),
CONEY STREET, York,

FOR

Morning Coffee,

4-course Lunch 2/-
(A Speciality).

Also

Dainty Afternoon Teas.

Grills served at Shortest Notice.

Private Parties Catered for
(For Tariff, apply to the Manageress).

OPEN from 10 a.m. to 9.30 p.m.

Comfort · Quick Service · Moderate Charges.

Picture House ad, 1929

and two floors up the restaurant café. It was THE cinema in York in those days. It was the number one cinema for Gaumont British in York, we also had St George's Hall and the Electric in Fossgate, so you had the first run of pictures.

The Picture House had been a silent cinema because it had the orchestra there. In the afternoons it was a shilling, and one and six in the circle, then in the evenings it used to go up to one and six in the stalls and two and six in the circle.

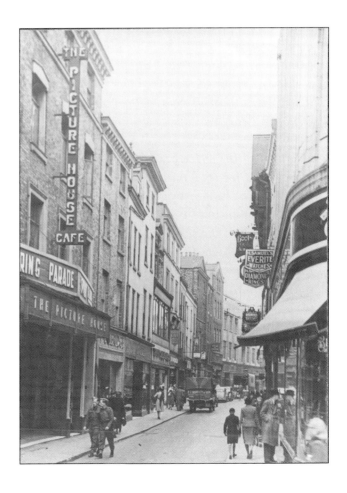

Picture House, 1940s
(York Oral History Society)

It was a very popular cinema indeed. I think the record audience I had was for a Shirley Temple film. We were running a kiddies matinée, starting at eleven o'clock, as we used to do on these big pictures. I came down to the theatre at half past eight and found the projectionist there, and my foreman and all the door staff. About half past nine the police came in and said, "You'll have to start running this film". "Why?" "Well, haven't you looked outside?" And there were kids right down Coney Street, just queuing. So we started showing films at about ten to ten. We just went on all the time, letting them in, and fortunately with starting earlier, they filled slowly and they came out, so we were at a continuous movement all the time. You never had trouble until you stopped queuing. They tell me that at seven o'clock at night the stalls queue was down to Ouse Bridge, from where Woolworth's is, and the circle queue went up to the Post Office in Lendal.

I just loved the entertainment business, I loved the cinemas. It was a hard job as a manager. We had to be in the theatre at half past nine in the morning, and then we ran continuously from about 12 noon to 11 o'clock at night. The first thing I did was to walk round the theatre to see that all my posters and everything were intact. The cafe manageress would then bring down the takings from the cafe, and the cashier would bring up the takings from the box office, and the girl from the chocolates and ice and cigarette kiosk would bring her money up. It was a rule with Gaumont British that if the manager hadn't banked the money by noon, a telegram was sent straight off to head office, because some managers had run away with the money. Then of course you were dealing with your staff, the cleanliness of the place, and also arranging publicity for the next film which came along.

In the Picture House there was myself, a cashier, a kiosk girl, six usherettes, a foreman, two doormen and I think six cleaners. Then three projectionists, chief, second, and the rewind boy. The staff had to do fire drill and the usherettes had to roll out the big hoses. And they behaved themselves, they weren't allowed to talk to each other. If we'd spot them they were in trouble. We used to have a foreman who was in charge of the doormen.

You had no choice of film. The booking sheet came along and told you what you were having. Then you had to work out time sheets of showing and all the publicity. We would do a tie-up with a firm. For instance I got about 50,000 milk bottle tops delivered because I tied up with Northern Dairies. And then their vans carried the posters along the side, showing the picture and name of the theatre.

Ernest had some innovative ideas when it came to publicity. At this time in York there were ten cinemas, all competing, and good publicity helped to ensure he packed the cinema.

In 1937, during race week, the cinema was showing 'Wings of the Morning'. He arranged for sandwich board men to attend the race-course and distribute leaflets made up in the form of 'racing tips'. On the outside it read 'Straight from the Horse's Mouth – take a tip from one who knows'. Inside it said, 'A sure winner – Wings of the Morning – running at the Picture House. Colours – glorious technicolour'. The following evening Prince Monolulu, 'the Prince of Tipsters', appeared at the cinema and attracted a big crowd.

In May 1937, a controversial film 'The Green Pastures' was shown. Ernest invited the Watch and Licensing Committee and clergy of all denominations to a special preview. (The film featured stories from the Bible acted by an all-black American cast. It remains only one of six films to feature an all African-American cast). With the invitations were artistic brochures asking for candid criticisms of the film. Interest during the screening was kept up by getting the local Press to print

Picture House films, 1945

(Yorkshire Evening Press)

extracts from the letters received.

In June, Ernest had 2000 samples of Pivers face powder distributed. On the front was printed, 'It is the wish of every woman to be beautiful, see beautiful Kay Francis in 'Sweet Aloes' this week'. The firm of Pivers also provided a display of powders and perfumes. This enabled Ernest to arrange tie-ups with three beauty salons, fashion and gown shops. The week before the showing of 'Good Morning Boys', a vestibule display was made with schoolboy howlers, a blackboard with lessons chalked on, and report cards. A pack of cards, dice and a dart board were also on show for younger patrons queuing to see the film. In August 1937 the Picture House featured 'O-Kay for Sound'. During the previous week, Ernest arranged for a local laundry to distribute 3000 hand bills in the parcels of people's washing. They read, 'The York Sanitary Steam Laundry is OK for Sound and reliable washing. For reliable entertainment see 'OK for Sound' at the Picture House'. He then negotiated a deal with the manufacturers of OK Sauce who arranged for 800 streamer bills in local shops with the slogan 'OK for Sound at the Picture House, OK for Sauce at Home'. 16 of the shops arranged a window display advertising the film, and sample bottles of sauce were given away to children. Ernest also secured the cooperation of a local grocer, where a number of complimentary tickets were placed in packets of Tipps tea. Cards were printed with a caricature of a bookmaker and, 'Mr Ceylon (the aristocrat of teas) Tipps O-Kay for Sound as a certain winner at the Picture House'.

In April 1938, the Deanna Durbin film '100 Men and a Girl' was showing, and Ernest advertised that he was offering prizes. The first prize, a Royal Enfield bicycle, was for the first person to send in a list of signatures of 100 men and a girl. The press described it as' one of the cleverest publicity schemes that's been hit upon for a long time'.

Ernest often got,

> *shop window tie-ups, and pages in the newspapers. All you did was go to the Yorkshire Evening Press, take your advert and they gave you the whole centre and then they got all the advertisers. Cook's travel used to have a big shop in Coney Street. Once or twice I had their window filled. They were all pleased to do it, the cinemas were THE thing in those days.*

> *We belonged to the showman's business, with the Kine Weekly. I was writing to America as well, and I got quite a few certificates for my showmanship in England. An enormous amount of time was spent on publicity. I loved it. We were always fighting against each other as showmen.*

> *We had to be on the floor between half past five and six o'clock in the evening. You were expected to say, "Good evening", to everybody who came in. And then when the film turned out, you were always on the front. I always talked to everybody I could because when you had three major cinemas, the Odeon, ABC and the Picture House, and the films were equal in strength, I got the*

extra people because they would say, "Oh let's go to the Picture House, Johnny's there. He speaks to you". And they came.

I'm a friendly type. It did help. These days you don't see the manager at all. Now he doesn't have much time to do anything except run the accountancy side. He certainly doesn't dress in evening dress.

Once they re-seated the Picture House, they were trying to get more seats in. They put 18 inch seats in. And I thought there'd be trouble. One afternoon somebody said, "There's a woman

Rear of Picture House and river (Ian Collinson)

been sat in the cinema for three hours and she can't get out of
her seat". So I had to go and rescue her. And then I had a word
with the head office. "My patrons are country people, not the
slim type. And I had one stuck in for three hours." And I was
most unpopular with my supervisor because we changed all the
seating back to 20 inch seats.

There was a lovely woman would come in, in the afternoons, and
she had her friend with her, they'd go up to the cafe and have a
meal. And then she'd give me a penny to call a taxi. As she went
out she gave the doorman a penny. This went on for a year and
a half. And it wasn't until I was leaving, and it got in the Press,
that I got a two-page letter from the woman, thanking me for
stopping the white slave traffic in the restaurant, and I suddenly
looked at the address, and she was a patient in the Retreat. And
the woman with her was a nurse. I'll never forget that woman.
She was beautiful and very polite.

The great earthquake picture was memorable. When we got the
films we had a cue sheet for the level of sound and the manager
had to sit in some part where there was a cueing buzzer, to give
you a buzz if you wanted the sound higher. And two buzzes if it
was lower. The cue sheet said, "When the earthquake starts, put
on full". This was in the afternoon and so we put on full, and all
the speakers blew. We had to keep the audience in the theatre, if
they wished to, for an hour and a half until we got the sound engi-
neers over from Leeds to replace the speakers and start again. A
lot of them stayed or we gave them tickets to come at a later date.

I liked the old musical films where boy meets girl, they fall out
and then they get back in love again and it all ends happily ever
after. The fantasy element was the thing of cinemas. You could get
stars, who would pack your house for you, I mean Fred Astaire
and Ginger Rogers.

The women used to love things where they'd come out crying, where somebody dies at the end. It was spoilt when we got to the kitchen sink dramas that started coming, when they got into this dreary sort of 'what life is like'. I know what life is like, I don't want to go and see it again.

War damage at the Tower cinema (York Oral History Society)

THE TOWER

In New Street, off Coney Street, the Tower Cinema opened in May 1920, but prior to that it had been the New Street Hall run by the Yorkshire Bioscope Company, the Palace of Varieties from 1908 and renamed the Hippodrome in April 1909, with seating for 900. The cinema suffered from incendiary bomb damage in 1942. It was the first cinema in York to install Cinemascope and Stereosound in 1954 but fell victim to television and closed in 1966. A year later it had been demolished to make way for the Davygate arcade. A Roman wall was found on the site.

CITY SCREEN

As early as 1997, the plan for City Screen London to open a multi-screen dedicated art-house cinema in Coney Street was made public. The London-based company bought the Yorkshire Evening Press building in Coney Street, the Press having gone to Walmgate. A lottery grant was applied for, to convert the building into a three screen cinema, coffee bar, restaurant and gallery, with computers available, a film and video suite and darkroom facilities. The cinema would also screen films which were linked to the national curriculum, such as Shakespearean productions.

City Screen before refurbishment in 2013

(Christine Kyriacou)

City Screen then went into partnership with York Film Theatre which ran the independent York City Screen at Tempest Anderson Hall. When the cinema chain was given its lottery grant of £2.8 million in March 1998, it was a record for the city, though they needed to raise more. Then in July, a 'mystery developer' stepped in with a donation of £600,000. Next door to the cinema would be a café bar, part of the Pitcher and Piano chain. Revolution and Orgasmic later set up bars there. The process of building the cinema on the old site involved decontaminating the buildings, cleaning up ink deposits and removing asbestos. The Kal-Jip aluminium sheets which were 23 metres long had to be shipped down the river to construct the new cinema. A crane had to hoist the sheets into position.

Lauren, Luke and Philippa Pinder, the author's daughter and grand-children, at City Screen, 2013 (Van Wilson)

In January 2000 the building was complete and screened its first film, 'Bringing out the Dead'. The auditorium was the first in York to be equipped with Lucas Film's THX sound system. As well as the films on show, there was an art exhibition by Adam Keay. A membership scheme was started up, which still operates, offering discounts, exclusive screenings and free programmes. The first month there were brand new films, together with old classics from the 1930s. Today the cinema is still very popular and offers special screenings and deals for mothers and babies, toddler time, children's club, people 'on the autism spectrum', and silver screen for over 60s. There is a regular comedy club, film quizzes and satellite showings of ballet, theatre and opera from London, Sydney, Paris, New York and Moscow. In May 2013 the cinema and café underwent a complete refurbishment.

CAFÉS

The Coney Street Café was next to the Black Swan in the 1880s, and the XL Café was at 54 Coney Street (now Burgin's). At 28 Coney Street, J Wanner ran a restaurant in 1911. These had all gone by the late 1920s when Miss Jessie Welch ran tearooms at 38a Coney Street. By 1930, this had become The Tea Shop, above Thomas Cook's travel office, and was advertising luncheons, teas and light refreshments.

THE WILLOW CAFE

Today the Willow is called the Willow Restaurant Bar and Disco. In the 1950s it was above the 'Fifty Shilling Tailors', advertising:

'Lounge now open for morning coffee 10am to 12.30.
Dainty Afternoon Teas
Grills and light refreshments from 6pm to 10.30 pm. Light orchestra from 8pm to 10pm.
Special arrangements for small dinner parties and theatre parties'.

Advert for Willow Cafe, 1940s

(Kelly's Street Directory)

John Avison recalls the Willow Cafe,

My mum and dad used to do their courting there. There was a very strict waitress who had the nickname Major Booth,

*after one of the founders of the Salvation Army. If she caught
a courting couple holding hands over the table, she'd rap them
over the knuckles with a stick, very strict.*

Chris Dowell recalls

*It brings back vivid memories of being a 15 year old, just
left school in 1954, and I met a charming young man down
Goodramgate who invited me to the Willow Café to have tea
before we went across the road to Burton's Tailor's. Underneath
Burton's Tailors there was a dance hall, the Court School of
Dancing* [before it moved to High Ousegate]. *We had a lovely*

Willow Restaurant, 2013 (Christine Kyriacou)

tea. I did most of the talking but John invited me to go across the road to Burton's. We learnt to do a jive, the quickstep, the foxtrot and waltz. There was no alcohol. You had to have orange juice in the interval. I had a nice circular new skirt, my mother had cut out on the kitchen floor, and stitched it round for me. I had petticoats to keep it out and I felt very grown up.

We were accompanied by his elder sister Bobbie who kept a good eye on us and looked me over at the same time. It always finished at a respectable time, well before midnight then he took me home. You didn't walk along Coney Street unaccompanied.

The Willow Café was lowly lit, tablecloths, nicely presented. We sat at a circular table for two. Very few people at that time because it was about half past six. They were very pleasant and obviously polite but left you to your own devices. It was mainly tea and cakes and sandwiches rather than cooked meals. I only earned ten shilling a week [as a trainee nurse].

You did have serviettes and tablecloths and nice cutlery. I felt that I'd been taken

Willow sign, 2013

(Christine Kyriacou)

out to tea which was a new experience at 15, especially after the war years because sweets and everything had just come off ration.

But the café changed and eventually became a Cantonese restaurant in 1973.

Suzy Brown remembers the Willow,

> *about 1970. You could dance there, and there weren't many places you could go later on and have a dance. It did have a bad name at times and we stopped going eventually.*

Today the Willow Restaurant, Disco and Bar is a late night venue which opens at 10.30pm until 4am and is for over 18s only, with an admission charge of £2.

Chapter 7

YORKSHIRE EVENING PRESS

The printing trade began in Coney Street as early as the 16th century. The Victorian History of England mentions that 'York's first printer, Frederick Freez, a Dutchman, purchased property in Coney Street years before appearing as a book printer in 1510'.

A printer named Thomas Broad issued political tracts from a house near the Guildhall in the 1650s but then moved to Stonegate.

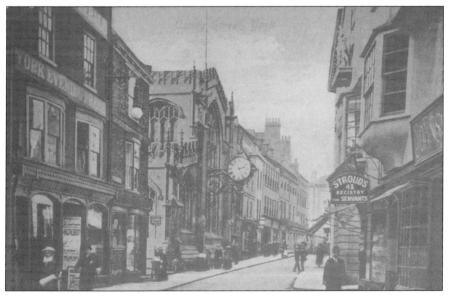

York Evening Press (on left) in 1900s (Ian Collinson)

The city's first newspaper, the York Mercury, was actually produced from Coffee Yard off Stonegate. But the York Courant, which began in premises near St Helen's Church in 1725, later moved to Coney Street, opposite St Martin's Church, into the premises which were originally the Bagnio or Turkish bath. Caesar Ward acquired the Press, succeeded by his widow Ann. She moved the business over the road next to the George Inn, previously known as Kidd's Coffee house. Ann Ward also published a number of books including the first two parts of 'Tristram Shandy'. Ann died in 1789, after running one of the largest printing establishments in the North of England.

In St Martin's Churchyard, one of the two visible gravestones, is to the memory of Benjamin Lund who died in 1808. He was clerk to the parish for 47 years but spent his entire working life at the York Courant, eventually becoming foreman of the printing office.

Benjamin Lund gravestone (Christine Kyriacou)

In 1815 William Hargrove bought the premises in Coney Street and the York Courant. In 1848 it amalgamated with the York Herald (of 1790) and was renamed the Yorkshire Herald. William Hargrove Junior joined the business as partner in 1856, and the Herald moved from being a weekly paper to a morning daily newspaper. In 1936 it returned to being a weekly publication and in 1954 merged with the Gazette to become the Yorkshire Gazette and Herald. The Yorkshire Herald Printing Works also published and printed books and other items.

Yorkshire Herald building before demolition, 1989 (Ann Gordon)

William Hargrove started the Yorkshire Evening Press on October 2nd 1882, as a four-page evening paper costing a halfpenny. He stated that, 'in local politics we will belong to no party and ever do our best to promote the wellbeing of the towns and districts in which we circulate'. The Coney Street premises were extended that year and new buildings added.

The building was a maze of passages, corridors and stairs. Staff were housed in small rooms until a new extension was eventually built at the rear which overlooked the river. The journalists were a close knit bunch and at one time were quite elitist. The printers were not allowed into the newsroom. There was a division between the two.

Many of those who later became reporters began their career with apprenticeships, not needing academic qualifications. In an article in the Yorkshire Evening Press in 1989, features editor John Potts recalled how, 'One flustered young lad who had taken a photo to the block-makers, for the next edition, put it down on the window ledge only to see the wind pluck it out, and started to panic. He ran down to the riverside to chase after it. That lad became a senior journalist with the Times'.

It was not until the 1980s that women joined the printing side of the paper. By 1990 a third of the reporters and many from the composing room were female. Prior to that, women had worked as front office receptionists, accounts clerks, secretaries and telephonists. Even up to the Second World War, women who got married were expected to resign.

The Evening Press relied on its street corner newspaper sellers in the city centre. Les Richardson was a well-known seller in St Helen's Square. He started at 14 and sold papers for almost 70 years. A post-card from America addressed to 'the Gentleman on the corner of Blake Street and Stonegate, York, England' easily found him. He greeted everyone with 'Good evening Lady' or 'Sir'. He would be given a cup of tea every day by Bettys and could be seen in his lunch break with his pipe by the fire in the Punch Bowl in Stonegate.

Les retired in December 1998 at 82. On his last day, customers queued to get a paper from him, and there was a ceremony in St Helen's Square when he was presented with a customised front page of the paper, and a cheque for more than £200 from his regular customers. His retire-ment present from the Evening Press was a new suit from Anderson's tailors. Press editor Liz Page thanked him for his dedication and years of service. As well as being mentioned in the York guide, he had also featured in American glossy magazines and was even interviewed on Sky TV news.

In the 1999 New Year Honours list, Les was awarded an MBE. When he travelled to Buckingham Palace in March, it was the first time he had been further than the North of England. Yorkshire Co-operatives gave him the VIP treatment with a trip there in a stretch limousine. For one day on 31 December 1999, Les came out of retirement to sell the final Press of the century. Applause greeted him when people saw him standing there. When he died in February 2003, the Evening Press sent a wreath spelling the words 'Press' in flowers, with a card saying 'To a true Gentleman of the Press', and tributes poured in from all over.

Les Richardson

(Yorkshire Evening Press)

John Avison worked at the Yorkshire Evening Press like his father before him. He was born in 1952.

I began my career at the Evening Press while still in school uniform, as a junior editorial assistant on a paltry wage of 50p for six hours a week. My duties included running errands for the sub editors working on the Saturday afternoon edition of the green Sports Press. I would compile cricket score cards which by a happy coincidence were typeset by my late father Frank. He

*joined as an apprentice in 1917, the newspaper he was to serve
for more than half a century.*

*In 1917 employment prospects for school leavers were poor.
With so many men at the Front, firms found it a struggle to
continue. A teacher at St Barnabas's School had spotted his
talent for English and suggested that here was a likely lad for
a job in newspapers. He passed a spelling and punctuation test
and was taken on.*

*The hours he had to work and the remuneration would make
today's school leavers shudder. The only days off he could
look forward to were Sundays, Christmas Day, and Good
Friday. And his pay? Just 5 shillings (25p) a week. His first job
was helping to check proofs. Gradually, he was taught how
to master one of the greatest innovations in 'hot metal' technology, the Linotype, invented in 1885, which cast a complete
line of type in one unit. The machine, with its keyboard designed
so that the most frequently used letters could be struck with the
left hand, assembled the matrices or moulds for the letters of the
words in a line of print, spaced them out to be the correct length
and cast a 'slug' for the complete line.*

*Behind the upper storeys of the Press office lay a labyrinth of
decaying, rat infested buildings, where the work was hard and
much of the equipment was primitive. In 1917 newsprint would
arrive by train and be brought from York railway freight yard
by a horse drawn dray. The goods access then was to the right
of the present passageway and was so narrow that the reels of
paper would scrape the walls as they were rolled down on a
bogie.*

*There were no familiar red Evening Press delivery vans. Copies
for outlying areas would go by train but generally newsa-*

gents collected their own bundles. One agent would walk back to Acomb with his. The contract to carry the Herald to York station was held by a local haulier, Harry Hawksby. His horse had been pressed into service by the army and he had been given a stubborn replacement, a mule. One night in the composing room, the cry went up, "The mule won't move. Any volunteers?" So the apprentice printers trooped out into the street. Some grabbed the spokes of the cartwheels, others tugged and pulled at the mule's harness. Even a bobby on the beat was drafted in. Eventually after much cursing and prodding, the creature broke into a trot near the Mansion House and the papers caught the train on time. The mule was not the only animal on which printing operations in Coney Street relied. The riverside location of the works made them a haven for rats, and the caretaker was paid so much a week to keep the company cat in milk and meat.

Frank Avison, second from right, Mrs Avison on far left (John Avison)

After six months probation, my father was told he would be given an apprenticeship which, in those days, lasted seven years. Apprentices had to 'keep good hours' and be home by a certain time. They were not to indulge in games of chance and, for some reason, even bowls was considered unsuitable.

The apprentices found themselves young men among many older men, as all those of military age were away serving King and country. The old timers would wear bowler hats, waistcoats and high choker collars. They were inveterate snuff takers and tobacco chewers, to counteract the fug of lead pots and gas mantles. The whole operation was steam powered, the rows of Linotype machines being driven by an elaborate system of belts and pulleys. A fan slowly revolving high up in the ceiling was the only ventilation in a room where, in summer, temperatures topped 100 degrees F. To get clean after a long inky day, printers washed in a bucket of water heated from a waste steam pipe.

The front page of the Yorkshire Evening Press comprised eight columns of closely typed small ads and personal announcements, including one headed 'Killed in action'. On the day my father joined the company, the biggest advertiser was Leak and Thorp, where 12 square yards of fine Wilton carpet would cost you £7-18s-6d. Another eye catching advert had been submitted by the De Bear School of 19 Coney Street, announcing, with commendable foresight and optimism, 'After the war, opportunities, train your girls and boys for the new business conditions".

The main war news was carried on page two, and conveyed none of the horror and degradation we now know existed at the Front.

The Evening Press had a tiny editorial staff of just three reporters, a chief sub editor and his assistant. The paper's only photographer, Bill Hull, was serving in the Royal Flying Corps.

Some messages came over the Post Office wires, and a stream of telegraph boys would go back and forth between the Press office and the York Sorting Office behind what is now Robson and Cooper's in Lendal.

One of my Dad's favourite printing anecdotes related to the London Times in the 1890s. The newspaper ran a report and included the sentence, 'Her Majesty Queen Victoria passed over Westminster Bridge'. Unbeknown to the paper, a mischievous compositor had transposed the 'A' in 'passed' for an 'I'. When the report came out, all hell broke loose across the Empire. But who was the culprit? No-one stepped forward so the entire composing room was sacked. After the incident, all lines of type on Linotype machines carried a unique indentation, a primitive bar code to identify the culprit.

One of the apprentice compositor's duties each morning, apart from pulling the mule, was to walk to Crow's butcher's shop in Spurriergate to collect a tray of meat pies. These pies, freshly baked, were brought back to the composing room and balanced on the edge of the girdling metal box to keep warm. Apprentices were given a daily milk allowance in the belief that it would suppress the lead in the system. Certainly there was a constant fug of tobacco, a lot of heavy smokers in the industry.

During the Second World War, the Evening Press had linotypes out in country areas in case the city was bombed.

During the Baedeker raid, the Evening Press offices were badly damaged. And the decision was taken that it would be published by the Bradford Telegraph and Argus. The Press's brass title piece, effectively its page one signature, with distinctive York Minster logo, was missing in the wreckage. My dad knew the composing room like the back of his hand and he was sent into the ruins and he found the title piece and it was brought back and sent to Bradford so the printing could continue.

John's own experiences many years later were quite different.

The Editor was a lovely chap called John White, he had very high standards. And I remember my dad went to see him and he said, "My son's interested in being a journalist". In a sense ink ran in my bloodstream because I was a sixth generation newspaper man, having followed my father, and my maternal grandfather into the industry.

John Avison (John Avison)

I'd been to Darlington College where we studied shorthand, obviously a vital tool, and also psychology and law, the English constitution, the rudiments of local government. After a week's initial training at Coney Street, I was sent out to the wilds of Selby to work as a junior reporter on the Selby Gazette. The great thing about journalism is the variety. You never really knew what to expect. In May 1970 at the height of the troubles in Northern Ireland, I was sent to Belfast to go on patrol with Yorkshire troops and I found myself in an armoured personnel carrier going into a fiercely Republican area of Belfast. And the vehicle was fire bombed while I was crouching in the back clutching my pen and notebook. By contrast I remember watching open mouthed as a Yorkshire vicar's wife stood in as a human target for a circus knife thrower to raise money for her husband's steeple fund. She survived the ordeal, but earlier that day, the knife thrower, who was balancing on a high-wire at the time, had his hand bitten clean through by the circus's dancing bear.

I was courting a Clifton girl, and I asked for a transfer back to the, I wouldn't say sanity, but back to Coney Street. I spent most of my time there as a general news reporter. About three nights a month I would cover the full meetings of York City Council with the legendary York journalist Stacey Brewer. We used to pride ourselves if it was happening in York, you could read about it in the Press. Another memorable assignment was in 1982 when the late Pope John Paul II preached to 190,000 pilgrims on York racecourse.

Our working day could start about half past eight in the morning and we could finish, if we were covering the York City Council, at half past seven at night. On one occasion, I'd been to cover 'The Exorcist' at the ABC in Piccadilly, a very contro-versial horror film. I remember walking back through the laby-rinthine corridors of the office in Coney Street, with the tick tick tock of the clock, and sitting at my Remington typewriter. I was tapping away merrily and my finger slipped between the keys, my wedding ring got jammed, and with my free hand I had to reach the telephone and dial 999 to get the fire brigade to come and release me from the typewriter. That building could be very very spooky in the middle of the night, having listened to people screaming watching 'The Exorcist'.

The way in was down a little yard between the Evening Press and Leak and Thorp's and through what were the bike sheds, and up a steep flight of steps. We had our own key. As a young lad I used to carry a two handled teapot up that flight of steps and I recall once, to my horror, getting to the top of the stair-case, and dropping the teapot when gallons of hot tea cascaded like a waterfall down the staircase.

We had chain smokers and pipe smokers. My wife recalls I'd come home from work and open my briefcase, and a little puff of smoke used to come out. It was passive smoking on a grand scale. Smoking was because of the pressure of deadlines. There's no wonder looking back that most of us repaired to the local hostelries at lunchtime. We had various favourites, the Punch Bowl in Stonegate, the Three Tuns in Coppergate, and if we were feeling very posh we'd go to the Judges' Lodging for Beaujolais nouveau.

I was given Am Dram, amateur dramatics. I also luckily got restaurants, the eating out column, because I was a bit of a bon viveur. I used to write a weekly Saturday night restaurant column. I covered all sorts, from pubs to Michelin star hopefuls, airports, even the humble roadside truck stop.

I remember characters like Viv Brooks. She lived in Rawcliffe. She was known for cycling along Bootham with two Pekinese dogs in a wicker basket. She had a distinctive umbrella hat, and she would go on the roof of the Evening Press and sunbathe.

Another well known writer was Chris Brayne, he served in the RAF and absolutely loved aviation. He was a member of the Yorkshire Gliding Club at Rufforth. He wrote the weekly feature column 'John Blunt'. In those days there was no company car. He used to cover his patch on a bike. Stacey Brewer was an excellent mentor and was awarded the MBE for services to journalism. He was famous for interviewing the Beatles at the Rialto in Fishergate.

The Evening Press garages, where the Austin vans were kept, were in Bootham Row, very close to Radio York. I spent many hours with a photographer in his grey Austin van in all weathers digging it out of snow drifts and all sorts. The one innovation that would have made such a difference to us was the mobile phone. But I spent most of my career standing in a wet smelly public phone box trying to get through to dictate to the copy typists in Coney Street. You would try to transcribe notes with a rather soggy notepad and a pen and pencil.

By that time, newsprint came by barge. In fact there was a strike in the 1970s by the National Union of Journalists, and it was decided to create Britain's first floating picket line. We assembled various canoes and dinghies stretched right across the Ouse from the Press to North Street, and this huge Scandinavian newsprint barge looming up. We were there with our placards. It didn't actually stop production but we did get a mention on the back pages of the Guardian for our efforts.

The journalists' strike of 1979 lasted for seven weeks, but the printers were out a lot longer, which meant there was no Evening Press for 13 weeks, and it took a negotiator to get the employees back to work.

One of the things I enjoy in the current Press is the column '100 years ago today', and '25 years ago'. I find some of the things that happened 100 years ago being reflected in life today. Certainly in terms of industrial life and disputes, nothing really changes. It's also gratifying to look at '25 years ago' and think, 'I wrote that'. In one sense your stories are almost like your children, you gave birth to those stories. You remember the blood, sweat and tears involved.

One of the most popular features of the Sports Press was the 'Spot the Ball competition'. I would go to the winner's house, get a picture and interview. We had one winner and when I arrived, I knocked and saw a shadowy form through the glass. I crouched down and shouted through the letterbox, 'It's John Avison, Yorkshire Evening Press'. A woman in a pink candle-wick dressing gown came. She said, 'Thank God, I thought it was my husband'.

I was responsible for collating all international and national news. It would come through a little hatchway from the wire room where the teleprinters were, my job was to prioritise the news and give the stories to the chief sub editor, which I thoroughly enjoyed. One of the dramatic changes was information technology, computers.

In 1984 computer setting and pasting-up of pages replaced the hot metal system. Within a few years,

the Press moved to Walmgate. At two o'clock in the afternoon we were still typing away on typewriters. We marched along Coney Street to Walmgate and started work with computers. The office was a very noisy place because we had the noise, the clatter and camaraderie of the composing room, and the noise of the presses, but also in the newsroom, the clank clank of typewriters. The atmosphere of Walmgate was almost like a bank, a very quiet tappety tap of computer keys. I missed the smell of the ink.

A lot of Evening Press men were very keen bowlers. They'd go to the Bert Keech Bowling Club in Marygate. I remember on my very first day as a little lad, at Coney Street, in my Archbishop Holgate's blazer, cap and tie, watching the sub-editors play shove ha'penny on the desk, and thinking, 'What fun-loving guys these are. This looks a fun place to work'. And it was indeed.

Malcolm Huntington

started at the Press in Coney Street on August 22nd 1949 and I stayed there until May 19th 1995, 46 years. It was The Yorkshire Evening Press, then it became Yorkshire Evening Press then Evening Press. It's now The Press. Initially, it was a private owner, Sir Ivo Thompson at Escrick. Then Kemsley's for a short time, then major owners were S Pearson and Son. Westminster Press were the newspaper side. Not long after I left in '95, Newsquest took over.

It now comes out in the morning the same as national newspapers do, rather than the evening. It used to have five different editions a day starting at 12 o'clock and finishing at quarter to five. One went to Scarborough, one went to Malton, one went to the East Riding, Pocklington, the city edition and the late extra. The late city edition we used to print at 20 minutes to four with the half past three racing results. Then the last edition was quarter to five.

At school my main interest was sport. The headmaster said, "You seem to enjoy writing compositions". And he suggested I'd like to consider being a journalist. I was introduced to the sports editor, Wilf Meek. He covered York City from the formation of the club in 1922 to when he retired in 1968. Then I took over in '68 and stayed till '95, covering a variety of sports.

Malcolm Huntington (Malcolm Huntington)

Now you go to university and get jobs that way. Then you started at the bottom, in my case as copy boy, basically running messages for the seniors, getting cups of tea, going to the post office for a postal order for the football pools. It was a very good grounding because you tended to learn about each department, the photographic department, the journalist side, the printing side. Now if you're a journalist, you sit behind a computer. I started with pen and ink in 1949 then went onto typewriters. There was only, I think, three typewriters in the building. The reporters had to share them. I was partly attached to the sports department. The sports editor would send me out on little jobs. The first job I ever did was covering the York table tennis championships at the Drill Hall in Colliergate in about 1951. The Press reporters used to go into Leak and Thorp at ten o'clock on a morning and have coffee in the restaurant.

Prior to this they gathered in the Picture House in Coney Street to write up copy on the way back from the magistrate's court.

It was the biggest sale per head of population in England. York then had about 100,000 people, now it's nearly 200,000 because they've taken in Dunnington, Haxby, Wigginton, Strensall and so on. We sold 56,000 papers to basically 100,000 people. Now of course with computers and websites, every newspaper in the country's circulation has gone down. I think the Press is currently about 30,000. Still quite healthy, seems to be doing reasonably well, which I'm delighted about. I'm not a lover of reading papers on computers. I like a cup of coffee and the news-paper in my hand.

I went from being a copy boy to being a junior reporter. Took shorthand examination, typewriting, English, English history. Worked my way up to senior reporter, then deputy sports editor, then sports editor, and finally chief sports writer, which I much preferred because I enjoyed the writing side of it more than the organisation. I retired when I was 61 after 46 years. I've grown up in York and knew a lot of people. When I retired the then editor said, "Would you mind writing about any sporting personalities who died?" At the same time, Yorkshire Post asked me, when I retired would I do York City matches for them. I've just completed 2000 matches of York City. When I was with the Evening Press I used to travel with the team and stay in the same hotel. We had the great advantage into the '80s of the green Football Press followed by the pink Football Press. When I became sports editor I decided that I'd like to see a lot more coverage of local sport. We went from five sports to 35. You had to wait for the green Press to know who'd won the football match. Now you've got television, computers, you can see the results five different ways. At its best it was the FA Cup match 1955. It sold 25,000 green Football Presses. That was one for every four people in York. On the day the Sports Press finished in 1983, we were on 3,000.

There was a billiard and snooker hall in Coney Street. Later on the editor at the time decided to make it into a sports hall [Ebor

Hall] *with a snooker table, dart board, for the staff. We played table tennis. We had the Yorkshire Herald cricket team, played on a Sunday* [as well as the Yorkshire Evening Press football team].

We had a lot of village correspondents. If you were at Bishopthorpe, Clifton, or the outlying villages like Strensall, we had a correspondent [who would send in their local interest stories]. *There were two rooms, one for seven or eight sub editors who look at the stories, put headlines on and précis them. Then the reporters' room, just a doorway in between. Before we moved from Coney Street, the partition was knocked down and it became one office. And then in Walmgate it was one big office, the editorial department.*

We could go home for lunch, an hour and a half. You started at nine and finished at five. Now people have a sandwich behind the computer, which applies to virtually every job in the world. Before computers, people used to telephone in their stories or write a letter to the news editor. And when the reporters were out on court service, in the middle of the day, they would telephone in their report. We had some very good typists.

The printing presses were right down in the bottom of the building. We used to go down for every edition and bring up half a dozen papers for the sub editors so they could make any changes for the next edition. They didn't seem to bother much about the noise and I can't remember anybody wearing ear defenders. When I was there initially, the ratio was carefully watched. It had to be 60% news and 40% advertising maximum. Obviously advertising pays for the paper. The paper was 2½d when I was initially there, now it's 50p or whatever.

We had the big Press Ball, tickets were like a needle in a haystack. All evening dress in the Assembly Rooms, that was the place to be seen. It was open to everybody, but it was run by the Press. The profits were given to charity.

I think we had two lady reporters and probably, going back to '49, '50 time, there might have been ten male reporters and two female. But as time went on, this changed quite a bit. In my later years the three main jobs on the paper were all women, the managing director, the editor and the news editor. And it was equal pay all the time I was there, which was unusual.

You worked odd hours and you'd get time off in lieu. In theory you worked 38 or 40 hours but in practice sometimes 50 or 60 hours, because you enjoy it. I found myself very privileged to be part of that. There's not many people can say they enjoyed the whole of their working life.

Arthur Winship was at the Press for most of his working life. He was born in 1931 and married Alma in 1955. She recalls,

He got in at 14. And had a lot of happy days. He did a late apprenticeship, we got married and wages were really poor. It was a three year apprenticeship and when he finished, he went to Cox and Wyman's at Reading for three years [from 1959–1962]. *It was when they printed Lady Chatterley's Lover. Then Arthur got chance to come back.*

All three of their sons, Graham, Kevin and David, worked at the Press at some time.

Arthur Winship as boy (Arthur Winship)

Graham did learn his trade at Noel Richardson's when he left school. Then he went to the Press office, then to college.

Her son David continues the story.

When Dad came back to York he was a stereo-typer, a plate maker, he was there until redundancy in January 1987.

Arthur Winship on far right packing papers at age 14 (Arthur Winship)

One of my memories as a child, he used to come home for dinner. He'd peep his horn on his motorbike when he came up the drive. When I came home from school for dinner, I never knew if he was going to be there. He could turn up in the middle of the afternoon. We never had a phone. They had breakdowns and delays. If I was in town and wanted a drink, we could pop in and see my dad, so I kind of grew up in Coney Street. We all had a Saturday job at the Press office. As soon as I hit 11 in 1977, I'd be there about lunchtime to half five. I got a bank book I opened just to put my wages in, £3 for one day. In '78 it went up to £5. I

Arthur Winship and the high speed rotary presses and sheet of flong (Arthur Winship)

Arthur Winship with Mick Broadley on left and Archbishop of York, Donald Coggan

(Yorkshire Evening Press)

was there about a year. Kevin was a bookbinder. When Graham went to the college I think it was typesetting and then he went onto computers.

On a Saturday I would come out of the actual office part, they had the brown swinging doors, and I'd go to the sweet shop for the reporters. One reporter liked hot peanuts. I remember going down to the basement. I used to hate it. There was the ghost story. Somebody died at the Press office, somebody who had worked there.

Many printers said they had seen the ghost, a man with a white moustache and wearing overalls, who was thought to be Bill Brittan, a print worker who died in the building.

There was a man in charge of us, Les Nash, there'd be a team of 11, 12, and 13 year olds. I was the youngest. It was an enormous room and it had loads of clocks on the wall. There was a dividing room, you could look through the glass, and the teleprinters were going with the latest football scores and they tore them off and put them in the dividing door. My job was to pick it up, roll it up, put it in this glass tube, and then it was like a suction system, it shot off. You could hear it going up into another room. The most important job was writing the football scores, if you made a mistake, that's what would go in the pink Press. My job was to get so many of the pink Presses and put them in the reporters' drawers. I think Malcolm Huntington, I'd get one for him. When I look back, it was quite a cool place to be, quite exciting.

A few years ago they had the residents' weekend, they had the Evening Press at Walmgate, so me and my dad went. As soon as I went into the printing place, I could smell it again, the

Sports prizes, 1980s; Arthur Winship far right at back (Arthur Winship)

printing was a unique smell. And very noisy. We used to say to my dad, "Why are you shouting when you talk?" Because at work they had to shout. They used to have blood tests to see if they had lead in their system. I remember them introducing things for their ears, but it was much too late.

They had a little room with a dartboard and a radio. I remember once they had a live eel, somebody had gone fishing and they were cutting it up, and the heart was pumping away on the table.

He said it was the happiest days of his life.

Yorkshire Evening Press press office being demolished in 1989 (Ann Gordon)

Today the newspaper is called simply The Press and it can be read anywhere in the world online. Catherine Suter, who was born in York, emigrated to California in 1980. She says,

I do read the Press every day. I keep in touch and know what's going on.

— Chapter 8 —
CHURCHES

ST MARTIN'S CHURCH

St Martin's, 2013 (Lesley Collett)

St Martin's, often known as St Martin le Grand, is an 11th-century church, mentioned in the Domesday Book and dedicated to St Martin of Tours, patron saint of soldiers. It is a little oasis in the busyness and bustle of Coney Street.

In 1437 part of it was rebuilt and the present tower was added. Once the Mansion House was built in 1725, St Martin's became the civic church, and was united with St Helen's Church in 1910. (St Margaret Clitherow was married at St Martin's in 1571 and her parents buried there. A service on the 40th anniversary of her canonisation took place in the church in August 2010).

Baptisms in 1814 show the varied occupations of men in the parish to include school master, saddler, linen draper, book keeper, tinner and brazier, chaise driver, carver and guilder, ostler, comb manufacturer, maker of fireworks, tipstaff, tea dealer, wine merchant, teacher of music and tallow chandler.

St Martin's was an important and beautiful church, though its parish was small due to the number of other churches in close proximity. In 1910 the feoffees (trustees) of St Martin's consisted of the vicar and churchwardens, and local businessmen and dignitaries including Samuel Border of Border's, Lord Mayor Robert Horton Vernon Wragge, Robert William Anderson of Anderson's tailors, and George Potter-Kirby of Kirby and Nicholson. In 1916 the altar and reredos were renovated to a design by E Ridsdale Tate.

By the late 19th century, there were few people living in the area. The 18th century two-roomed St Martin's Cottages, which had stood in the alleyway beside the church to house poor widows and spinsters of the parish, had become unfit for habitation by 1950 and were later demolished. The vicarage with its garden and greenhouse, which had stood behind the church, was knocked down and a house in Bootham became the new vicarage.

The darkest part of its history was when in the 1942 Baedeker air raid on York, the church was almost destroyed, leaving only the south aisle and bell tower. Fortunately the stained glass windows had been removed in 1940. During the raid, about 9,500 properties were damaged or destroyed, 72 residents killed and many injured. Firewatchers from the neighbouring Evening Press office rescued the ladies from the cottages. The scene was one of horror as shops and houses burned in the street, with St Martin's, like the Guildhall, a smouldering ruin. Even the following morning, the street was awash with molten glass and debris. There were those who thought the church should not be rebuilt, despite an average Sunday attendance of 300, but the feoffees and wardens launched a campaign to raise funds for its restoration, and York City Council helped.

St Martin's Blitz, 1942 (David Wilson)

The church was restored by architect George Gaze Pace between 1961 and 1968, and is considered to be one of the most successful post-war church restorations in the country. Part of the site, to the right of the original church, was left open as a memorial garden, enclosed by railings. A new organ was a gift from the German people. The jewel of the church is the magnificent window featuring St Martin, with its five lights and 20 compartments, which was put in the church in 1437, and is the largest window in any parish church in York. It was originally the west window, but when the church was reordered in 1967 it was placed in the newly-constructed transeptal tower, so on opening the heavy oak door, the visitor immediately faces it.

St Martin's bell mechanism by Newey (Mike Race)

The main external feature of the church is its clock which overhangs Coney Street. A clock has existed there since the 17th century. The bracket was built by Thomas Cooke, who was based next door to the church, at a cost of £180 in 1856. The naval officer above the clock, the Little Admiral, dates from 1778. The clock was made to strike the hours and quarter hours and, in 1925, chimes were added by George Newey of the York firm of Newey and Son which began in the 1880s. The clock was damaged in the air raid and the hands stopped at the very moment the incendiary bomb hit. It was rebuilt in the 1960s by the Neweys, the only turret clock to be designed by Roland Newey, George's son. Unfortunately the bells were stolen in 1960 but one new bell replaced them, weighing half a ton. The gilded head of Father Time was a copy, as the original was burnt. Geoffrey Newey, George's grandson, who started as an apprentice at 14 and became known as York's 'Father Time' said that his favourite clock, of all the ones he maintained, was that of St Martin's. He said it had taken a whole year of his life in the 1960s. In 2011 the bracket was found to be suffering from corrosion and needed to be stripped and rust proofed. When the clock was removed, Coney Street was closed for nearly five hours as workmen took it down using a cherry-picker. When the clock was returned to its place, having cost over £54,000 to repair, it was rededicated by the Archdeacon of York, the Venerable Richard Seed.

Edward Bacon is now responsible, with three others, for the clock at St Martin's.

Two years ago on the retirement of Geoffrey Newey, I formed, with three other people, the York Clock Group, to take over the winding duties that Geoffrey performed in York. We currently do about eleven clocks, including St Michael's. That was stopped for a long time but we made sure it was working. We do them once a week.

Rev Jane Nattrass and Little Admiral
(Derek Ralphs)

Edward Bacon on the roof with the clock at St Martin's (Mike Race)

I became interested 40 years ago. I bought an old clock at an auction sale, at Crampton's in Toft Green in the 1960s. Fortunately there wasn't much wrong and I made it go. So I went along the next week and bought another one. The second one wasn't quite as easy. That's how I got to know Mr Newey because eventually you come across something you can't tackle yourself, so you use a professional. And we became great friends.

The dial and brackets had been taken down after the war and were replaced in 1966 when Geoffrey built the present mechanism of the clock. There was corrosion and it turned out that the mask between the dials, Father Time, which was wooden and gilded, had rotted inside. The gilding on the paint looked fine but the inside had virtually disappeared. It is now cast in resin, so is more permanent.

Yorkshire Evening Press staff help to reinstall the bell in St Martin's, 1962: Arthur Winship and Brian Ellis second and third left.(Yorkshire Evening Press)

The Little Admiral, as he is affectionately known, rotates every 24 hours. The instrument he's holding follows the sun, as does he. On every hour when the clock strikes, he spins round, a complete turn.

The clock was made in 1966 and was one of the last of its type to be built, probably the last, which has a cast flat bed, is weight-driven and hand-wound with that type of mechanism. When people wanted a clock on a new building, they would install an electric. There aren't [many clockmakers] now, it's a result of the lack of apprenticeship schemes in the '70s and '80s. But there are now courses at universities and colleges to train clockmakers.

There are three sides to the clock. The time side records the passing time and is more often recorded on a dial outside the building, there's a striking side which strikes the hours. Sometimes it will strike one at the half hour. The third part is the chiming part, which will chime the quarters on a series of bells. The striking and the time side, each needs winding up. The time side is 125 turns, and the striking side is a little bit more and a little bit heavier. There's a big crank handle, a bit like a water mill. The chime was composed by Andrew Carter. The very common ones are the Cambridge chimes, like Big Ben, Westminster clock chimes, and they're often repeated.

The people who did this clock were the Cumbria Clock Company, owned and run by Keith Scobey Young. He has worked on the Westminster clock, and he completely rebuilt the clock at Hampton Court Palace. There are about two other similar-sized companies in the country that will undertake to look after these clocks. I think a clock like this one will hopefully be running forever. There are no more to be made, we should look after the ones we've got.

Rev Jane Nattrass is the current minister of St Martin's.

I look after five churches, St Olave's, St Martin's, St Helen's, All Saints' and St Denys. My mission is to see God at work in the city centre. On a Sunday I will do two or three services. The clergy team and the readers move around the churches. St Martin's holds services on a Wednesday and a Saturday. The church has a growing congregation, it has a very clear idea about peace and reconciliation. It occasionally has a service on a Sunday. Easter Sunday for example we have a chocolate fountain, hot cross buns and an Easter garden.

Rev Jane Nattrass and Pastor Robert Pfeiffer, April 2012

(Derek Ralphs)

We had a service on the 29th of April 2012 to mark the 70th anniversary of the Baedeker raid. The weather was atrocious and people turned out and packed that church. We'd also become a partner in the Community of the Cross of Nails.

We had Pastor Robert Pfeiffer from Lübeck, because that church in Lübeck bombed in the war is a partner in the Community. Robert spoke some German in the service, and he's firmly of the opinion in such services that the German language alongside the English language is very much a sign of a continuing reconciliation.

We had a German intern from Coventry Cathedral, also bombed during the war. [Mary Peacock, one of the firewatchers actually on duty on the night of the air raid, read a 'Reflection'.] *And Canon David Stone from Coventry Cathedral presented us with our Cross of Nails which now sits in St Martin's. York celebrating 800 years of its charter was a motivation for us to do something.*

When Coventry Cathedral was bombed, the cathedral was destroyed and afterwards they used timbers for a cross for the service the next day. But also, the nails from the roof were collected by a man and he began to make crosses out of them that were given to people. So this Community of the Cross of Nails has grown over time. It's a worldwide partnership. When they came to give us our Cross, the following week they were going to Dachau. We used words that every church in the part-nership will be using, the Litany of Coventry Reconciliation.

After the service we had refreshments in the Guildhall and the pastor came round to my house. And he met a couple on the street and the woman asked if he was Robert Pfeiffer and told him about her father [who had been an RAF Bomber Command pilot. She asked him to shake her hand in the spirit of recon-ciliation]. *Robert sat here and told me the story and he was so moved. For him that is how peace and reconciliation works.*

The older generation remembered the bombing and the fires with great excitement. And that surprised me really. You do wonder how it stays with people. There's somehow excitement amongst it all, and actually they're still alive and everything's all right. The stories of the fire-fighters and everything are moving to hear.

We have a great team of bell-ringers across this city. It mattered to us that the church bells were rung that day so that people in the city would know something was happening.

If you look on the floor there's a piece of slate and it's the Cross of Nails in there and it says, 'Father forgive'. That's always been in St Martin's. And when I saw that, it all made sense to me, it all came together.

Memorial stone by George Pace (Lesley Collett)

The King's Book was signed by the King in Buckingham Palace in 1921, a list of York people killed in the First World War, made of oak and weighing nine stone. It was presented to the Minster and then was transferred to St Martin's in 1938. It was restored in 1990.

There is also a memorial book in St Martin's, of people who died in the Baedeker raid. There was a line, 'To the unknown German aircrew'. As part of the commemorations, we had that book updated so the calligraphy includes the names of the German air crew.

It's important that the George Pace work is recognised. We're looking at how he interpreted the courtyard and at opening it to the public to be used for peace work. There's an anniversary of George Pace coming up in 2014.

We have peace vigils, we put a candle in the courtyard and a lantern. The week that six soldiers sadly died from the Yorkshire regiment, we had calls from people about them, and people tied flowers to the railings. We put an Easter garden in for the first time in 2012, and it made people stop. It's a corridor of shops and this huge church sits there but sometimes Coney Street is extremely busy and this is a stop. Every time we go into St Martin's there is somebody in, either tourists, or people who've just gone in simply to be quiet. Peace and reconciliation work continues, and everybody's presence at that service meant that we were all saying that there is hope.

On 29 April 2013, the church held a Lighting of Lanterns gathering to remember the casualties of the air raids of 1942 and to celebrate the first anniversary as a partner in the Community of the Cross of Nails.

Memorial Garden at St Martin's (Mike Race)

ST MICHAEL, SPURRIERGATE

A church stood in the place of St Michael's Church in Anglo-Saxon times. The oldest parts of the church are the pillars from the 12th century and it has stained glass from the 15th century, but it was largely rebuilt in the 19th century. The reredos, which displays the ten commandments, was made by John and William Etty in the 18th century. The clock, thought to be the oldest in the city, was moved from the tower, which was demolished in the 1960s, to the outside of the building in Low Ousegate. It had been installed in 1896 by the Newey family. A new belfry was created in the shortened tower and the tenor bell hung in it for chiming by an electric hammer. In 1968 there was a full restoration of the peal of six bells, re-hung in fittings in a new cast iron and steel bell frame.

Between 1872 and 1931 the 'curfew bell' rang each night at eight o'clock. When the Lammas Fair was held in York, it was also known as the Bishop's Fair as the Archbishop of York had jurisdiction over it. The commencement of the fair was heralded by the tolling of the bell at St Michael's. The sheriff then symbolically handed over authority to the Archbishop and his bailiff. The fair ran for two days, ending at three in the afternoon the day after Lammas Day (August 1st), when authority was handed back to the Sheriff. During the fair, the Sheriff had no power to arrest anyone in the city.

There are memorials to four Lord Mayors in the church – George Mancklins, 1666, John Wood, 1682, William Whytehead, 1741, and Francis Stephenson in 1783, as well as two sheriffs, Peter Richardson in 1687 and Richard Sutcliffe in 1784. Interestingly, the font in St Martin's Church has the name of Richard Mancklins, churchwarden in 1717, embossed on it.

St Michael's closed for worship in 1935 when the parish was united with St Mary, Castlegate. It became redundant in the 1970s. York

Archaeological Trust carried out an excavation in St Michael's prior to the Spurriergate Centre opening in 1989. It initially seated 90 in the restaurant but was refitted in 1998 and again in 1999 to increase its capacity, and the upper deck, the Cloisters, was opened up. The restaurant has space for 150 people, and there are two shop areas and a quiet space.

Spurriergate Centre, 2013 (Christine Kyriacou)

Joan Sargent came to York in 1990 and started work at the Spurriergate Centre in 1991. Fifteen years later she studied for an MA and wrote her thesis on the Centre.

> *The centre opened as a small enterprise, a tearoom, in a redundant church on a main shopping street, not anticipating its*

*potential. It was overwhelmed by the initial response and
unequipped to serve all its customers in the first year. It relied
heavily on volunteer staff. After the first year it was necessary
to completely replace the servery area and to consider how it
could become a vibrant and robust business.*

*It appealed to me because it was a church with a difference. The
people of St Michael le Belfrey had a vision of a Christian centre
in York. Some of the funding came from them, and the Diocese
and from the Feoffees of St Michael Spurriergate, who look after
the fabric and the building.*

*There was already a strong manager, Sylvia Wilkinson, who
really pioneered and helped to get it started up. They advertised nationally and somebody from Spurriergate who knew me
invited me to apply, and after a long process, they appointed
me to be pastoral co-ordinator of the centre. It was about us
being a church in the 20th century. We saw ourselves as a Christian community so we prayed for our customers every day.
We weren't there to bang people over the head but to listen to
people and to make this restaurant a really good experience.*

*We have a mission statement. To share God's love with the
people of York and its visitors, in the way that we served. We
had some paid staff, lots of volunteers, giving the best service
we could. The second part was to offer a listening ear. All the
staff and volunteers were trained in listening skills. The counselling service came a few years later. As you begin to listen to
people, you listen to some really big issues. I remember a lady
who came in, her husband had committed suicide and she was
looking for help and support. And we were able to get her some
professional help. But we also continued to listen to her and
support her and her children.*

Joan Sargent (Joan Sargent)

We were looking at extra premises, they came available next door over the top of Thomas the Baker. We set up a professional counselling service and offered it to people who perhaps couldn't afford it [so they gave a donation rather than fees]. *Quite a number of us trained at York St John.*

The third part of the mission statement was to have an emphasis on justice in trading. So we developed a Fair Trade shop, and all our tea and coffee is fairly traded. Fair Trade at that point was new. We were at the forefront of trying to push it, and support projects like Water Aid. Then the fourth bit of the mission statement was to share the good news of Jesus Christ. How do we do that? It's about offering the other services but also developing book groups, the Alpha course, Bible groups, knitting groups, Powerpoint presentations, children's activities, all sorts of groups, supporting other organisations in the city. It's very much about being involved in the community.

Local church leaders started doing a prayer breakfast once a month. We would invite the head of the police or the head of the council, the head of tourism, to ask them, "What are the needs in the city and how can we as church leaders support that?"

One of the biggest things, on the tables we invited people to leave prayer requests. We've been amazed because every day people do. One couple used to come and kept leaving prayer requests, saying, "We can't have children. We're going down the adoption route". We got to know them, and I remember the day they brought their child in, it was fantastic. That's being church in our modern world, that's happening in Spurriergate. We became people's family. People with mental illness, marginalised people. One lady used to come five days a week and have the same meal every lunchtime. If she went on holiday she'd send cards and letters, we were family. When she died, we had a memorial service for her.

The business is not incidental. There's Spurriergate Trading Ltd, the business side, and St Michael's Trust charity. They work hand in hand. Because we were offering a listening ear, different organisations would contact us and say, "We've got people with learning difficulties or different issues, we'd like to put them on a placement". We've also worked a lot with one of the local prisons so we've had people coming back into the community. York Carers Forum might do an evening there, we might promote them for a few weeks, have things round the walls. We also rent out some of the offices, such as SASH, Safe and Sound Homes, about getting vulnerable young people into safe homes. We support Carecent with food, Family Matters had offices in Spurriergate, and we help Reflect, a pregnancy crisis service.

Kirsten England, head of the council, came to speak at Spurriergate and they invited a number of us to sit in the council

Spurriergate Centre, 2013 (Christine Kyriacou)

chamber looking at the needs of the city. That's been really exciting. We don't want to proselytise and aggressively bang people over the head with the Bible. When you look at the history of York and you go to the council chamber and you see pictures of what happened centuries ago, a lot of the stuff that happened in York came out of the churches. The hospitals, the education, that's our history and our inheritance. It's not perfect and it never will be but we've been able to break some of the barriers down.

Spurriergate is moving into a new phase. [They have just agreed a new 50-year lease] *with new activities such as evening concerts and Monday night café for students, particularly from overseas.*

The Centre now acts as a consultant for similar projects around the country. Hugh Bayley, York's MP, used the Spurriergate Centre as the venue for his campaign to increase aid for Africa. The centre sees about 3000 people through the premises each week from all walks of life, and has won awards for the quality of its food and child friendliness.

We're not the only ones who are concerned, many people in York are caring people with a lot of heart. That makes our city tick. Coney Street is an important street, where the council chambers are and for the churches to sit in, it's important stuff that.

Plaque marking the opening of the Spurriergate Centre, 1989 (Lesley Collett)

S. BORDER & CO.

Tea Merchants, Coffee Roasters,
Italian Warehousemen and Foreign Produce Merchants.

We invite an inspection of our numerous specialities in the following departments :

BAKERY

Cherry and Genoa Cakes, Macaroons, Pork Pies, Hunting Nuts, etc. The above freshly made daily.

We draw special attention to our TEAS, which are skilfully blended to suit the water of the district. Our ORIENTAL TEA at 1/7 per pound is unsurpassed as a Family Tea. (Special quotations given for quantities, carriage paid).

TEA

CHINA TEA. The Medical Profession are strongly recommending the use of pure China Tea. We have two excellent Teas at 2/7 and 1/11 per lb. respectively.

COFFEE

Our COFFEES are carefully selected from the various growths and great care taken in blending to produce the best possible result. They are roasted and ground daily on the premises.

BAKING POWDER.

We prepare a very excellent article (guaranteed to be free from any injurious ingredient) from an original recipe. Packed in tins at 9d. each, or 10d. per lb.

A trial of the above is respectfully solicited, as they cannot fail to give satisfaction.

49 and 25, CONEY STREET, YORK.

Border's advert (York Directory)

190

— Chapter 9 —
GROCERS *and* PROVISION MERCHANTS

Coney Street and Spurriergate have always been the home of grocers or provision merchants. In 1823, Richard Brown was a confectioner and tea dealer and Robert Foster ran a tea, coffee and fruit warehouse. At 7 Coney Street, Thomas Watterworth was an agent for 'the sale of genuine teas' and a cheese, flour, salt, bacon, butter and ham factor. In Spurriergate Robert Ellis and Thomas England were both bacon, cheese and ham factors, and John Elliot was a wholesale and retail confectioner, pastry cook and Italian warehouse. His Christmas advert offered 'Ornamental game and goose pies sent to any part of the kingdom'.

By 1872, these businesses had all closed. Number 7 Coney Street was occupied by William Wilson, provision dealer, John William Triffitt was a confectioner at 16 and at number 47, Mary Ann Craven was a confectioner who went on to have a sweet factory in York. In Spurriergate there were two fish and game dealers, John Aspinall and Henry Hewison.

Hamilton and Hall were based at 25 Coney Street by the 1870s (before the Picture House took over the premises in 1914), advertising as 'grocer, Italian warehouseman, wines and spirits'. An Italian warehouseman stocked goods from Italy, such as olive oil, pickles, pasta and certain fruits.

BORDER'S

Samuel Border came to York in 1867 to live with his uncle, the grocer John Winn at 38 Coney Street. He became a partner in 1874, and the business was known as Winn and Border, but he was sole owner when his uncle died at the end of the 19th century. Samuel became a councillor for Monk Ward in 1881, Sheriff of York in 1887, and Lord Mayor in 1898. He was briefly Lord Mayor again in 1907 when William Bentley died in office, Governor of the Merchant Adventurer's 1892 to '94, Governor of Bootham Park Hospital, Director of York United Gas Company, Chairman of the Grand Yorkshire Gala in 1906 and York Pageant in 1909. He died in 1911 aged 61 in Devonport, and his body was brought back by the Great Western Railway at a cost of one shilling a mile for carriage, totalling £17-14s. His funeral cost £60-14s-1d including 2 guineas for tolling Great Peter at the Minster.

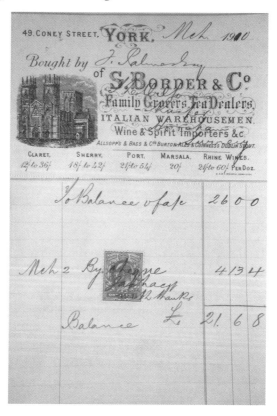

Border's invoice (Alan Powell)

Border's continued after Samuel's death but closed at the end of September 1960. It was bought by a London firm but demolished in February 1962. A Roman wall and tower were unearthed during demolition.

Alan Powell worked there in 1953.

Samuel Border had one son, Edwin George Border, (Mr George), the senior partner when I was there. Peter Border was George's son. Then there was a Mr Leslie Border, a cousin.

On Alan's first day he

reported to Mr Frank Hollins in the order room. I started learning what the commodities were and where they were all kept. The travellers went out, brought the order back, or sometimes customers would pass their orders in.

Butter was loose, used to get the big barrels from Lurpak. They weighed about a hundredweight. It took two of you to lift it up onto the counter. We used a butter wire and proper butter knife. Tea was loose, they blended their own, there was Indian and Ceylon. They roasted and ground their own coffee in the warehouse at the back. The green beans came in sacks hoisted up to the top floor. A chap called Kenny roasted it up. Occasionally people would ask for whole coffee beans, but by and large they were ground up as and when required.

Fresh coffee was sold in ring packs, half a pound or a pound. If anybody wanted a quarter pound it was a flat pack on a sheet of paper you had to fold it up. Sugar came loose in hundredweight bags. Before my time, it came in a cone, they used to have to break it off.

Bacon was fresh, from Harris's at Carne. There was a wire net cage of very fine mesh, and the bacon was hanging in there. The air kept it dry and cool, it was fly proof. Plain bacon, smoked bacon and the full sides with a hock and the shoulder and the middle. That was taken down to the provision counter, boned out, and sold as necessary. Cheese was all loose. Just after the war, all you could get was basic mousetrap Cheddar. Then

we started getting English Cheddar, New Zealand Cheddar, double Gloucester, white Stilton, blue Stilton, Cheshire, Wensleydale, Caerphilly, Gorgonzola, Gruyere, Emmental, Parmesan, Neufchatel, Tomme de Savoie. That was covered in grape seeds. And a Norwegian Gjetost, a goat's cheese. The cheese had to be turned every two days so the whey would work its way through it and it didn't dry out at the top and bottom. All the cheese was wrapped in muslin or, if it came from New Zealand, they were coated in wax to preserve them. Any cut parts were covered with greaseproof paper to preserve it overnight.

There was the shop front, four windows with a central door. Inside to the left was cakes

Alan Powell (Alan Powell)

and bread brought in from George Ilee and Son in Front Street, Acomb. One of my favourites was strawberry flans. Tiptree was the main jam we sold. There was full fruit, high fruit and fresh fruit standard. Same with tinned fruit, that had various grades. And that depended on the amount of sugar.

195

Underneath was a big cellar, and a machine to bottle wine in. There was a big caged area where the wines and spirits were locked. We had the cooked meat counter run by Wilf Beal. We used to sell glass jars with D shaped tongues in. There was three big hams in a wire or metal cage, and they'd be boiled. After so many hours, we'd lift them out with cloths, lift the wire cage out and put it into a hot box, stainless steel, double thickness walls, insulated. You'd leave them to cook overnight.

Mostly they were boned out when we got them in. But occasionally if we were out of stock, they'd take a ham off one of the sides of bacon and bone that out, truss it up, put it in. Once it was cooked, the skin was taken off, and coated in orange breadcrumbs. It was beautiful. Proper boiled ham, all the stuff nowadays is injected with water. At Christmas we'd get pigs' heads in. Above the counter at the back was a stainless steel rack with hooks on and pigs' heads would be hanging up there.

Border's café sign on left (Ian Collinson)

Border's advert

They sold a lot of continental sausages, German Knackwurst, Lieberwurst, Shinkenwurst, and then Italian salami, and Danish salami and French I think. And tongue and beef and roast pork to sell as slices. We sold Symington's powdered soups.

During the war that was one of my lunches when I went home from school, Symington's oxtail soup. Then Cross and Blackwell's and Heinz tinned soups and Baxter's. Campbell's came in later. On one occasion Knorr Swiss set up a little cauldron at the end of the grocery counter and started making soup out of their powders and they gave us all a free sample. Margarine was national margarine still, though we got a Dutch one called Stagg. Then Echo and Stork eventually came in. We started selling Chinese stuff. Bean sprouts, water chestnuts, lychees, kumquats, all tinned. There was one lady who kept cats. She'd buy six tins of salmon and a tin of crabmeat every week for them. Salmon during the week and on a Sunday chopped up crab, 5/6d a tin. In the '50s you were talking quite a lot of money.

At the back was the china. It was Royal Cauldon. I used to buy it for my mum for birthdays and Christmas presents. They sold glasses as well, French crystal.

There was always a seasonal display in the middle, Chinese figs, Muscatel raisins in triangular whitewood boxes, almonds, French glacé fruit, orange and lemon slices. And Christmas crackers. We used to get Tom Smith's, the person who invented crackers. They were gorgeous, absolute works of art. On Christmas Eve we'd be called up into the accounts office one by one. There'd be a bottle of sherry and you'd be given a glass. That was it.

At the end of March we'd do stocktaking and everything in the warehouse was weighed. Lentils and dried peas and split peas, all these came in big bags. And fine oatmeal, coarse oatmeal, medium oatmeal, all kept in tins. On the day of the stock check all the tins were weighed, all the tins of soup counted after the shop closed. We all had to work late, until half eight, nine o'clock, whatever. They always gave us tea, provided by the café. Our morning tea and coffee, that was right at the top of the building where we had a staffroom. There was various teas. They had their own blend, gunpowder leaf tea, Lapsang Souchong, Darjeeling. The only member of staff from the café who used to come down every morning was the typist, and she'd type up the menu. That was put in the entrance way in a little brass casing.

I counted about 43 staff. You had five or six in the order room, where I first started. That's where the soap and the soap powders were kept. Camay was the big one. When I used to

Visitors to York will find every convenience at

BORDER'S
CAFÉ and GRILL ROOM

Refreshments daintily served at moderate prices.

S. BORDER & CO., LTD.,
TEA MERCHANTS,
ITALIAN WAREHOUSEMEN,
CAFÉ PROPRIETORS and
FOREIGN PRODUCE MERCHANTS,

48 and 49, Coney Street, York.
Telephone 2938.
Branch at MARINE DRIVE, BRIDLINGTON.
30

Border's café advert

go dancing I could always tell which soap a girl had used when I danced with them. Camay, or Lux. I don't know whether it's a benefit of working in a grocer's shop!

Peter Border sat in the middle, and he could see all parts of the shop at that one point. There was a stand at the bottom with a pillar going up with mirrors on it.

There were travellers that went round. Joe Bannister rode a BSA Bantam, and there was Vera Mann and Bob Leadley. All you had was your order book, receipt book and your pen. That's all you needed, and the gift of the gab. When I eventually got promoted to doing the travelling, I started going round on my bike. Later on I got a van to drive. Monday morning, my first call would be St Aubyn's Place, St George's Place, the Horseshoe, Middlethorpe Drive, then St Helens's Road, the Archbishop's palace in Bishopthorpe then Mrs Peter Terry and Mrs Dodsworth.

On Saturday morning, I worked on the provisions with Joe Bannister. You had a white smock and a white apron tied round your waist. Bob Leadley worked on the grocery counter with Mr Medd and Mr Jones and Mr Ewbank. They wore a shirt, tie and jacket, and a white apron. With the licensing law, they could only sell wines and spirits between certain hours. Whisky was just coming back on the market after the war. Vat 69 and Teacher's Highland Cream, White Horse, Haig's Gold Label, Haig's Dimple. There was a ladies' hairdresser [nearby]. *The ladies would ask for beer shampoo and they'd send one of the lads round to buy a bottle of beer for the shampoo.*

In New Street, there is a gateway [to the back entrance]. *There was a basement with steps down to it. It was quite a reasonable sized yard. Loose vinegar was stored there in a barrel. You'd have to go out on a cold winter's day to get two pints of loose vinegar. The warehouseman was Bob Morrow, an Irish man. And he swore blind it was haunted by Roman soldiers. He wouldn't go down there at night.*

One of my customers was a member of the Multiple Sclerosis Society and they had an event and wanted 20 Christmas hampers making up. We did that for them. And another customer was Mrs Raylor of the scaffolders in Copmanthorpe, and Lady Deramore, there was quite a lot of the county set.

It was a great job, I really enjoyed it. They were good bosses. When I became a traveller, I got commission, a penny in the pound.

But the day came when supermarkets made it impossible for the grocer's to continue, as Alan recalls,

they called us all into the board room upstairs. There was a big portrait of Samuel Border on the wall above the fireplace.

Mr George and Mr Leslie smoked pipes and it was thick with smoke in there. They said, "The bad news is we're going to have to close, we can't compete".

Eileen Kelly (née Perkins),

was born at Thorganby in 1938, about ten miles out of York. I started work at 15 at Border's, 1953, I was there to '59 or '60.

There was two men that went out and got orders off customers, all over the place, like Haxby, Wheldrake, Elvington, Acomb. They were Ernie Bean and Don Millward. Two van drivers delivered the orders, Herbert Snowden and Malcolm Grassit. A lady lived in our village, Lady Dunnington Jefferson. Her husband was Sir John and he had a lot to do with the Yorkshire

Border's coffee roaster (Alan Powell)

Border's Royal Cauldon teacup (Alan Powell)

Show. My dad worked for them and she'd ring the office and say, "Would Eileen bring me…?", usually cooked ham or cheese, and I'd take it on the bus.

For the tea, there was a piece of paper and it had Border's stamped on it, and you'd put the loose tea onto this and fold it up and pack it. You can imagine what loose tea was like on one piece of paper. You mastered it in the end but it was just practice.

There was a gardening department, a man called Mr Hare, sold seeds, equipment, potato and onion sets. Beyond that there was an office with three ladies. I became friendly with one, Elaine.

Mr Ewbank was in charge of wine and spirits. When I got into the shop a bit more, I'd often help him. I got quite good at knowing what wines were, and different whiskies. Dorothy Howe was in charge of the biscuit counter. The biscuit tins were all along a rack, tilted so you could easily get into them. Rich tea, custard creams, fig rolls, everything.

There was another long counter I often helped out in, with a great big till, with a handle you pulled down. There were tiny drawers, in them were herbs, spices, loose pepper, loose salt, cardamom, paprika, lovely when they were all together. All with brass handles.

I'd maybe only been there two years and I got a bit bored, so I got a job in a newsagent's at Goodramgate.

Eileen Perkins, now Kelly (Alan Powell)

It was so dull, I couldn't stand it. So I picked up my pride and went and asked for my job back. I started the week after, just like that. Mr Peter was getting a fresh fruit and veg department going. He asked if I'd like to run it with him. I thought that was lovely. Frozen foods were just coming in to being, Findus. He got a big fridge at the side. Every Monday I would go with him up to Piccadilly to Burley's fruit and vegetables, now Banana Warehouse, or Simpson Brothers in Swinegate. He would show me what apples to choose, and all the fruit. That would be delivered that afternoon or next day. I would polish all the apples and make a nice selection. Once I was weighing some bananas. I had brass scales and I polished them till they shone. Something clattered into the scales and in the bottom was the biggest hard backed beetle, it had been in the bananas. I just dropped them and ran screaming into Coney Street. Mr Beal came out. I said, "There's something in the scales".

While I was in this department, there was Katherine Worsley that became Duchess of Kent. She would come in for fruit and veg, with her hair in a ponytail and a dirndl skirt on. She was very friendly. The Mansion House sometimes wanted fruit and veg delivering. I would put them in a box and wander across the road. I often saw Mr Simpson or maybe it would be the cook. They never invited me to have a look in.

Mr Peter got a new car once, it was a Mayflower. They were all looking through windows. To get a car was something. In summer Eunice Bradley, my friend, and I would ride our bikes from Thorganby into York. We were only 18, 19.

I had tonsilitis and I always seemed to get it in winter. One year I was in bed three weeks. Herbert did the country orders, and he brought this big bouquet of flowers and a basket of fruit for me. And it cheered me up. And they'd all written on a card.

I thought what a lovely gesture.

I only got about £7 a week and out of that I had to pay my bus fare, board and lodge and there wasn't much left for a bit of pleasure which was cinemas really. We didn't go clubbing! We didn't eat out at all. But you were happy.

Nina Smith worked there from 1946, when she was 15, to 1953. From school, Nina had been sent to the jeweller's, Hopper's in Coney Street. The choices for a girl at that time were in retail, or

there was a lot of people would go to Rowntree's or Terry's. I was at Hopper's a few weeks. Threading broken necklaces, that was my job. It was horrible. Then I went to Border's, I started in the order room.

I eventually went in on the cooked meats. Audrey Pulleyn was on the biscuit counter. She'd say, "Just come upstairs and I'll show you where t'biscuits are for Mrs So-and-so". All fancy biscuits, some lovely biscuits, chocolate three-cornered things.

Peter Border lived on Tadcaster Road in a big detached house. They invited some of us to go and have a game of tennis. We went two or three times. I remember old Mrs Border, George's wife, she was a real jolly homely woman, no airs or graces, used to make us a drink. Then they had a hammock. I remember thinking, 'They're posh', and years later I got one of my own.

Food rationing was still on when Nina worked at Border's. Some customers 'tried it on'.

Quite a few people used to say they didn't get the butter or other rationed stuff in their order. So after that we had to double check these orders, made sure the stuff had gone in.

It's your word against theirs I suppose. I remember the Judges Lodgings. They always got plenty, got more than their rations. I suppose it went on all over.

Nina Smith at 17, in the Jane Russell blouse (Nina Smith)

Three of us decided we wanted more money so we went to Woolworth's. It was a bit more money there. And they gave us half a crown a week rise to keep us [at Border's]. *17/2d a week I was getting at first. I had about three outfits all through my teen years, couldn't afford anything else. I'd got a white Jane Russell blouse, you could have it off the shoulder or draw it up. It was 30 shillings and I paid a woman on the market half a crown a week, a lot of money. I wore it with different skirts.*

Nina recalls that it wasn't all business.

I used to go dancing. Audrey Pulleyn used to teach me how to dance up in t'rooms [at Border's]. *Quickstep and rock and roll.*

205

Madge Glew from Cawood, her son started work when he was 16, the only lad there. He once got a big brown bag, he took it into the shop and blew it up and banged it. It was like an explosion, everybody scattered.

There was always a queue on the cooked meat counter. And I remember great big things of smelly cheese. Willie Walker used to get this wire cutter and cut it all up. He was a real joker. He'd been in the war and he used to tell us how they'd be doing route marches and see rotting bodies.

I got married but I left to get more money. We both went on the buses and doubled our money. I was getting £3-10s when I left at 21, and on the buses £7 plus overtime.

Nina and Jack Smith 2013 (Nina Smith)

LIPTON'S

Anne Sains recalls her father's employment at Lipton's grocer's at 34 Coney Street.

He was born in 1900. He would be in his late twenties when he was manager. He worked for the Co-op in County Durham then went to Sunderland and worked for Lipton's and then came to York. It was quite a big private firm. Sir Thomas Lipton was well known.

At the back it ran alongside Judges' Court, the little alley. There was just a single doorway and there was a solicitor's firm in the yard at the back. There was a well in the back yard which we all knew about. When the new stores took over [in the 1960s] *there was a great song and dance because they found this well, but Dad knew it was there, though it was capped off.*

I remember being taken to the shop and standing on a stool and weighing sugar into blue bags and tea into little packets. I was about eight or nine. One of the earliest strong memories was the morning after the Blitz in 1942. My father had been on fire watching duty, because he wasn't in the services. I assume he was a reserved occupation. He also didn't have the best of physical health. We were at home in Scarcroft Road. I remember my mother carrying me down, and when we got there, the policeman at the end, he said, "It's all right, I've seen him". (They were the regular policemen and they all knew Dad). I remember a fireman lifting me over. They had the great big canvas hoses all over the street. Father had had a busy night. They'd had incendiaries on the roofs. The store had a flat roof. I know he found like a miniature hot air balloon on a wire frame. I don't know whether they floated incendiaries with them or what. He was fire watching with Mr Jones who was manager of Halford's , they lived over the shop. Quite a few people lived over the shops at that time.

I remember counting food coupons. Father used to have to bring them home on a weekend. They had to go into bundles of 10 then 100, to the Food Office on a Monday morning in the Assembly Rooms. If you didn't have the coupons, you couldn't account for what you'd sold. I learnt to count, counting food coupons. I remember a big flag on a flagpole out of the bow window for Victory Day.

Coney Street was father's life. They had to do a certain amount of stocktaking every night. He was home Thursdays usually at half past eight, and Fridays and Saturdays could be 9 or 10.

It was one long counter and they had a cash desk with a pulley system. My father used to cut the bacon, the sides of bacon used to hang in the back shop. Once it had been cut, it had to go in the freezer. Then downstairs the first cellar was great big cheeses. The smell was very strong. Beyond that cellar was another which went under Coney Street, where they'd keep all the paper bags and brown paper. The store cat lived there. You needed them [for mice and rats]. It was so close to the river. They used to say that these cellars connected and went through Leak and Thorp down to the river. When they had these hoses for the fires after the Blitz, there was Water Lane by the side of Woolworth's, and that's where they were getting the water from. There was so much rubble near the Press office, they couldn't get that way.

They had all the glass-topped biscuit tins on a metal rack. Things were piled on the counter, made into patterned pyramids. And very full shop windows with bakelite price stickers. Now they're all wrapped and chilled. They had their own cocoa and

George Sains at Lipton's (Anne Sains)

*their own tea. You can still buy Lipton's tea. They had a roll up
blind. You had a pole and you pushed it back and brought it out
to protect the food from the sun.*

The shop took deliveries on

*carrier bikes. A bit like 'Open all Hours' and Arkwright's bike.
They were wrapped up in brown paper and tied with string.
My father was brilliant at tying parcels. The only vehicle I
remember was one from the railway, a three-wheeler thing with
a trailer.*

We didn't get any perks, because it was rationed and allocated. I remember mother saying we could do with some bacon and father saying, "You've used your ration". He was the one who'd eaten it. You went shopping every day. If word got round that they were going to have rabbits at the fish and game shop, the children were sent to queue on a Saturday morning. Then mother would come with the sixpence when she thought you'd be near the top of the queue.

Dad's never flooded, but then of course the river was dredged regularly and there was a lot more river traffic. Much more depth to the river. They used to dredge it and tip it on to the hilly fields up near Terry's factory. The Picture House was popular, and it had a café. If you joined the Red Cross cadets you could go in there cheaper on a Friday night.

There was a man, I never knew who he was, he used to sit on a chair while he was being served, he used to take a piece of paper, fold it in half, and cut things out, fairies and rabbits, and give them to Dad for me. I painted them white and put them in a frame on a black background. He once did one out of a half-penny stamp, and it was this little fairy.

There was one priest from St Wilfrid's, used to go in for his tea and butter. He was in his 90s. He was Polish and he'd come over with the free Polish. When Dad's store got a liquor licence, he'd come with an attaché case and hand it to Dad and he'd put a bottle of whisky in it. He was a lovely man. Used to wear a little black homburg hat and a black overcoat.

Self-service supermarkets were coming into fashion. His shop was too long and narrow. There was no room to make exit tills. By that time, associated suppliers included the Maypole, Home and Colonial and the Meadow. They gave dad three weeks notice. After 40 years! It was never a well-paid job, and in the latter years the manager was paid on turnover, and the staff were paid a set wage. Father wasn't earning as much as I was in an office. All the hours he put in!

He was 62, so no redundancy pay and no prospect of getting a job as far as he could see. He went to the Co-op in George Hudson Street, just simply to do bacon and cheese. He spent the last three years of his working life there.

Once supermarkets became common, there were no longer any grocer's or food shops in Coney Street. In 2013, Morrison's is about to open a small shop in Spurriergate. Catherine Pickard remembers that

British Home Stores used to have food counters in the '70s and I'd get honey roast ham and a vanilla slice. They had a lovely meat counter, it was known for it, my Dad would go there to get ham shanks. It was a sad day when it stopped selling food.

CROW'S BUTCHERS

Many people remember Crow's in Spurriergate, which also had a branch in Walmgate. (See also Catherine Suter's story of Crow's in the chapter on fashion houses). Malcolm McManahan went there.

I remember in the window the long strips of polony in red packaging and black pudding in black. We used to eat quite a lot of it, though once I found out what the black pudding was made from, I didn't eat it anymore. The penny ducks were nice. Back then you didn't question what went into them, though I assume there was no horse meat. I couldn't eat one now but when you're young you didn't question things. You either ate it or had nothing.

6   YORK CITY YEAR BOOK.

CROW BROS.,
(LTD).

Pork Butchers,

Spurriergate.   -   Walmgate.
Townend Street. Heslington Rd.
Acomb.

BUY QUALITY.

His sister Catherine Pickard recalls that

It was famous for its penny ducks. They were tasty. It was 'unspecified' meat mixed up with potato and onion. You'd get a square of it and they'd chop it up into slices and fry it. They'd say you'd eat every part of the pig except the grunt, and that would be in the penny ducks.

Crow's butchers

(Kelly's directory)

— Chapter 10—
BOOTS *and* WOOLWORTHS

BOOTS

Boots began in 1849 in Nottingham where John Boot sold herbal remedies. After his death, his son Jesse took over and expanded the business. Qualified pharmacists joined to dispense medicines. In 1920 Jesse sold the company to the United Drug Company of America, though it was later sold on. The introduction of cosmetics, photographic and optician services increased its success. In 2007 it was bought by AB Acquisitions Ltd.

Boots opened in Coney Street in 1919, the medicated wine licence being transferred from J S Liversidge, who had been a chemist previously. The shop had been built in 1900 in the medieval style.

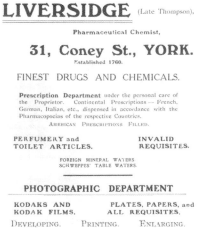

LIVERSIDGE (Late Thompson),

Pharmaceutical Chemist,

31, Coney St., YORK.
Established 1760.

FINEST DRUGS AND CHEMICALS.

Prescription Department under the personal care of the Proprietor. Continental Prescriptions — French, German, Italian, etc., dispensed in accordance with the Pharmacopœias of the respective Countries.
AMERICAN PRESCRIPTIONS FILLED.

PERFUMERY and
TOILET ARTICLES.

INVALID
REQUISITES.

FOREIGN MINERAL WATERS.
SCHWEPPES' TABLE WATERS.

PHOTOGRAPHIC DEPARTMENT

KODAKS AND
KODAK FILMS.

PLATES, PAPERS, and
ALL REQUISITES.

DEVELOPING.   PRINTING.   ENLARGING.

Telephone 513.

Liversidge (York Shopping Week 1910)

Boots subscription libraries were introduced in 1898, initially with second hand books. By 1903 there were 143 Boots Booklover's Libraries. Membership was 10s 6d a year, or 2s 6d deposit for each book taken, with charges of one penny a week. Some of the libraries, in London for example, offered tables and chairs, sofas and potted palms. The books on offer were 'healthy and wholesome', and mostly romantic fiction for ladies. By 1938 there were 35 million books a year being exchanged. As the cost of paperbacks dropped, and public libraries (with borrowing free of charge) increased their stock, subscription libraries began to wane in popularity. In 1961 W H Smith closed the libraries in their stores and Boots took them over, but they too closed in 1966.

Timothy White's was a dispensing chemist, which started in Portsmouth in 1848. In 1935 it became Timothy White's and Taylor's and opened a shop in Coney Street after the Second World War. In 1968 Boots took over the 622 stores though they kept the name for some years.

In 1983, the Coney Street branch of Timothy White's and Taylor's became the Boots Cookshop. Boots itself had a facelift in 1986 costing £400,000, during which the Cookshop was closed and relocated to the main store. The rear entrance was in Market Street, and the shop occupied two floors. By 2001 there were branches in Acomb, King's Square, Coppergate and Clifton. In 2001, a drop-in health service opened. The store moved to the site vacated by Woolworth's in 2008. The building which housed Boots until then is now occupied by T K Maxx.

Joan Moat was born in 1939 and worked for Boots in Coney Street from 1954 until 1958.

When I left school, I applied for three jobs and I was accepted for them all. I chose Boots because it was the most money. And it was popular. Lots of people that I went to school with went there. When you went for the interview, it was the territorial manager, he would always look at your maths. I was good at mental arithmetic. People thought you had a good job if you worked at Boots, one of the better shop jobs. I got £2-4s when I started. We'd get a rise every year.

Joan Moat *(Joan Moat)*

Upstairs was the library, and we had a little bookshop which went into Market Street. We sold cards, mirrors, suitcases, there was a handbag department, jewellery, toiletry department, then a drugs department, surgical, baby stuff. We used to sell methylated spirits. You could go in with your bottle and fill it up. And vinegar, you'd take your own bottle and they would fill it up for you. Lots of us used to get sore hands, and they used to make up their own potion.

Everybody was called Miss, Mrs, Mr, no first names at all. The manager was very strict and you always had to look busy even if you weren't. When I went there I hated it, long days, aching legs and feet. But I did get to like it very much. You only became a senior assistant when you had been there a lot of years. I was on stationery most of the time. When you came in from

Market Street, stationery was straight below. It was very cold and draughty when the doors were open. The pen department was on one end and the table stationery on the other, such as greaseproof paper, doilies, serviettes, table mats. You were just plunged in at the deep end. Everything was dusted, you even dusted pens. Ridiculous really. Everything was wrapped up in brown paper with cellotape, no paper bags. So if you got two articles that were totally different shapes, you did two parcels. It was all adding up in your head and you gave little receipts for everything. At the end of the month, everything was checked, to make sure you hadn't any mistakes, and if the takings didn't add up to what was in the till, you were reprimanded.

The manager was always on the warpath. Making sure you were doing your work, and, "Oh this is out of place, just tidy this up", and there'd be nothing the matter with it. Wednesday was half day. And on a Wednesday morning, sometimes you wouldn't even get a customer, it was so quiet. You had a more personal approach, you knew more about the goods you were selling. You knew prices without looking. We wore overalls, tied in the middle, horrible, blue. Then after a couple of years we went onto nylon blue ones. If you were on the pharmacy or drugs, you wore white.

I have two friends now whom I met at Boots in the 1950s and we're still good friends. We used to have nights out, go to the pictures, or swimming baths on a Wednesday afternoon. The staff rooms were level with the clock above the library. There were three floors. You used to do stocktaking once a fortnight, then when you'd been there a few months, you had to do the ordering yourself. The manager was a stickler, if he heard you say, "I'm sorry I haven't any", he'd be on your back, "Why haven't we any?" We used to have a gentleman that had been shell shocked. He always went to the library for his books. He was a regular customer, two or three times a week, and he wore a bowler hat, a white silk scarf, and a black overcoat. He was a familiar figure in York.

I did spend some time working in the bookshop and you were expected to read a little bit. We did a lot of children's books, high quality ones. We used to do well particularly at Christmas. Christmas time we'd so much stuff you couldn't move. The shop was decorated. The porters did that. The four porters did any packing if there were big items. They'd deliver goods if they could go on a bike, there wasn't a vehicle.

We had men on the drugs department and the dispensary but there were no [male assistants] *working on any of the other departments. We had a qualified nurse there, in a white hat and blue uniform. The territorial general manager, Mr Murray, was a lovely fella. He lived out at Collingham so when we had the Christmas party at Bettys, I'd get a lift home with him. We'd two fulltime window dressers and they'd do something different each time. Singer Sewing Machines had a little shop nearly opposite. You'd see ladies sat in the window and they would be mending stockings. And Jaeger, that was very upmarket. It was so expensive they didn't put prices on things.*

Boots clock (Van Wilson)

Saturday was the big day. We all used to get a bit more dressed up, big earrings on and made ourselves look more present-able. Trying to get a Saturday off was just awful. My sister got married and you would have thought you were asking for the earth.

*I think there would be 80 staff at least. We had a little kitchen
so you could warm things up on the cooker. We had a lady
there called Dorothy, she was a little bit backward but she was
lovely and would do anything for you. You'd take your food in
half cooked and ask her to put it in the oven. She was employed
up to two o'clock, she kept the kitchen clean and tidy and
helped out.*

*I do remember a friend of the manager's would come in. He
might come with two £1 notes, newish, stuck together and
he was just testing you. You'd say, "Oh you've given me two,
did you know?" And that was your test, in case you kept it. I
remember one girl being sacked. She'd been pilfering money, two
shillings here, five shillings there and they caught her.*

*When I married, I moved to Boots at Harrogate. I stayed there
until I was six months pregnant.*

Joan Sadler bought an oval mirror from Timothy White's which now
hangs on her living room wall.

*I bought it 50 years ago. I said, "I won't be able to carry it
home." They said, "Well we haven't a delivery service, but if
you tell me where you live, I'll bring it myself".*

You got personal service. And in Boots when Mr Gration, [the
father of TV presenter Harry Gration] *was there, he was always
around helping customers.*

Malcolm McManahan recalls Boots in the 1970s.

*I remember buying our first record player from the electrical
department in Boots. The first single I bought was 'Far Far*

Away' by Slade, from Boots. It was in a picture sleeve. The record department was on the second floor. Further back were the LPs, and by the till at the corner it had a rack on the wall with the singles in the chart order each week.

I'd go in every week. I didn't get a single [a 45rpm vinyl record] *every week because they weren't particularly cheap. 45s were more durable but still prone to damage. Because they cost so much money, you handled them with great care.*

The toy section used to have a rack which displayed View-master slides. A little kind of hand projector and the slides were circular discs. You had about seven or eight little images that would rotate when you pressed the lever down. I can only remember them being available at Boots. They had factual things and views of cities and countries but also TV and film related. The first slide I got was Thunderbirds. When you're young, and it's a 3D image, it's kind of magical and that never leaves you.

At that time there were several record departments within a small area. W H Smith's, Woolworth's and Boots all sold records. There was also Bostock's which Malcolm McManahan remembers as a

discount record shop in Coney Street. I don't think it was there very long, but I used to go in an awful lot. Once I got my first single in '74, it triggered some desire in me to collect them. They'd sell singles for half the amount that you would pay for a chart single. I used to go in quite a lot and it was always busy. I assume it was the singles that didn't sell well, so once they dropped out of the chart, they would just sell them off to get rid of the stock.

WOOLWORTH'S

F W Woolworth was founded in the USA but Frank Woolworth opened the first British store in Liverpool in 1909. Within five years there were 40 stores. By 1953 there were 800, and by the late 1960s there were 1141 branches.

The York store opened on 8th November 1924. When the Picture House next door closed in 1955, Woolworth's was modernised and enlarged to take over the old cinema. The cafeteria was very popular in the 1950s and 1960s. The store was again modernised and refixtured in July 1972. The restaurant closed but the store announced that refrigerators and televisions were to be sold.

In 1986 the store closed for several weeks for a half a million pound facelift. But in September 1987, all fulltime staff were told that they were to be part-time. In June 1988, the store was fined £200 for opening on a Sunday. Another refurbishment took place in 1993, costing £1 million and a branch opened in Monks Cross in 1998. The store celebrated its 75th anniversary in November 1999 but the next few years were difficult ones. The store which 'sold anything and everything' finally closed in January 2008.

John Avison's

> *abiding memory is the weekend when hula hoops came into fashion. I remember as a little boy walking along Coney Street, seeing all these teenagers shimmying out of Woolworth's.*

Alwyn Cammidge was born in 1935.

> *I must have been about twelve, I had a friend, Reg Macmillan, who was older than me and Reg was working at Woolworth's, doing odd jobs, clearing rubbish away. He told me there was a*

job going. Two years after I'd been there, they brought a law out that said you had to be 14. They kept me on and paid me out of petty cash so it wasn't on record.

We went to work after school, we used to walk from Park Grove. We'd break cartons down because there was a carton recovery firm, CRS, come round and took all the cases away. We used to break them, fold them up, bundle them into different sizes. They had an old hand baler, we'd fetch that down, tie it up, bale the paper and waste. Then we had to sweep the whole of the store. On a Friday which was the late night, we used to have to Bond Seal it, which is a sealant for all the wood floors. They had to be spotless and clean. We had big brushes. Two foot wide, and soft because of the polish. You gradually worked your way till you got downstairs where the stores were. I had to work till it was done but only got paid for two hours.

In them days there was a cafeteria, bit like an American-style cafeteria, with all chrome. There was a cellar where every-thing was kept and replenished. We'd take stuff in wickerwork baskets so they could fill the racks up. One of the perks of the job, sweets were on ration and girls used to clip them out with scissors. They was all over the floor. We used to collect them and take them home and give them to our mates. The stuff that was rationed, biscuits and sweets, were in an enclosed area which was locked all the time, except when we had to go and fill our baskets to take them upstairs.

There was a hierarchy, like a floor walker, assistant manager, deputy manager and so on. I got on well with the assistant manager, Mr Radkey, who lived in Harrogate. He had a big motorbike. He used to go grass track racing. He'd say he would take me, but we never did get round to it.

It was quite a happy place. They used to have cats to keep the vermin down. I remember one time a cat having kittens in the top of a box of glass. Some was broken and all the little kittens was being lifted out slowly.

Peter Pigott (Janet and Peter Pigott)

When it flooded it used to go in the warehouse. The food was always above the water. But the glasses and stuff was always at the bottom. If something had to be recovered, we'd get overtime for it.

The marketing side of it was well thought out. Because the cafeteria was at the back, an L shape above the river, people had to walk through the store to get there.

Coney Street was a busy street, throngs going down it. There was wagons and all sorts delivering at the same time.

Peter Pigott was a student at St John's College in 1958, after being a medic in the RAF.

The main attraction of Coney Street was Woolworth's. It was ideal to buy oddments when I was a poor student. I remember the street always appearing busy. In those days cars and bicycles used to go up Coney Street from Spurriergate to Lendal and St. Helen's Square. People used to step off the pave-

ment in front of them. I was always wary that someone might get hurt by doing so and I'd have to be called upon to use my medic's skills! There were a lot of near misses at times, especially involving cyclists with pedestrians, but no-one was ever hurt badly enough for me to be involved, thank goodness.

Catherine Pickard

went to Woolworth's every week. One week they were doing a demonstration. The lady had this doughnut maker with a deep fat fryer and she was making all these doughnuts. I asked my mum if I could have a doughnut making kit. We didn't have a deep fat fryer and I tried to do it in the frying pan and all I got were these little round bits of hard batter.

You'd go there for clothes, pots and pans, homeware, bedding, and they had a record department. There was the cafe at the back, all formica tables and it was the in place to go when you were a 1960s teenager, with drainpipe trousers and beehive hairstyles. I was ten in 1968. There were all these metal seats, swivel stools, all very mod. Sugar jars with the scoop, you'd lift it up and you'd get one scoop of sugar out. Apparently there was a frothy coffee machine and that's what attracted them.

What's missing now is the excitement. You'd go into a record shop and if they had the record that you really wanted, and you could listen to it, it was

Bag from Woolworths record department

(Mike Race)

all about the anticipation. And then talking about it with your friends, looking to see what other people were buying, what was popular. It wasn't just downloading something on the internet, it was a whole experience.

Malcolm McManahan recalls Woolworth's

had a wide entrance. As you walked in, there were little containers with various types of biscuits, pick and mix and you could choose what you wanted. Then they'd weigh it. I remember the ones with lemon icing, we used to get them every week.

I remember getting The Saint annual in Woolworth's. There was a section about the Beatles 'Yellow Submarine' that would date it to '68 or '69. I was a big fan of The Saint. I bought Queen's 'Bohemian Rhapsody' in the record department in 1975.

About Christmas 1971, I got from Woolworth's one of those assembly kits of a Frankenstein model, a bit like Airfix, and they specialised in horror figures like Frankenstein, Dracula and the Wolf Man. You put the figure together then you'd paint it in luminous colours so it glowed in the dark. And there was a skeleton one, and the Forgotten Prisoner. They kind of dealt with things of the macabre which must have appealed to me when I was young!

Coney Street had character then. It's kind of very stereotypical now. It's lost a lot. It's been standardised so you can't tell one city centre from another. I suppose it's progress in a way. Everything through a computer, but you miss out on something.

— *Chapter 11* —
W. H. SMITH'S

Henry Walton Smith established his book and stationery business in London as long ago as 1792. His youngest son William Henry continued the business which became W H Smith & Son when his son, also William Henry, joined in 1846. The business increased and in 1848 they began to open the famous bookstalls in railway stations. The Smith family actually continued to be involved right up until 1996. Along the way they owned several other chain stores, such as Waterstone's until 1998, Virgin Group and John Menzies. The company also has shares in Yorkshire Television.

As well as its branches at railway stations in the UK and some countries overseas, it also has shops at airports, bus depots, motorway service stations and hospitals. The stores in the USA and Canada were subsequently taken over, leaving shops in France, Denmark and Sweden, Australia and India. Smith's is in the process of setting up branches in China.

The York shop of W H Smith's started out at 13 Coney Street, taking over from John Sampson, book and print seller, stationer and newsagent. Sampson's business included a subscription library in 1901, a department of the Christian Knowledge Society, and then became Ordnance Survey agent. By 1920 it had become Smith's.

The fire that started at Leak and Thorp in January 1933 had a huge effect on Smith's. The glass roof fell in and the basement flooded. Their entire stock of stationery, and 30,000 books were ruined, with a loss estimated at between three and four thousand pounds. But like its neighbour, the shop was up and running in a few months.

Fire at WH Smith, 1933 (Yorkshire Herald)

Fire damage at WH Smith, 1933 (Northern Echo)

Fire damage at WH Smith, 1933

John Avison recalls W H Smith when he was a teenager in the 1960s.

I used to go to the Court School of Dancing in High Ousegate. This was well before the days of 'Strictly Come Dancing'. I got as far as the cha cha cha but didn't progress from that. What I would then do, to give myself a little treat, was to get a hamburger in the Wimpy Bar in High Ousegate, and then go to WH Smith's downstairs to listen to a single. You would choose a record, and be directed to a booth. One day I chose the Beatles 'Twist and Shout' EP, brought it home, played it on my old Dansette record player and my dad went mad. "Go and take it back", he said, "Get something else". I went back and bought 'Steptoe and Son' EP. But certainly W H Smith's was packed with teenagers all clicking their fingers. You went into little tiny booths with graffiti on the side like 'Terry loves somebody else'.

Catherine Pickard's mother worked in Smith's in the 1960s.

My mother cleaned the offices and kitchen. She didn't actually clean the shop floor. I think that must have been people on a night. She worked Monday, Wednesday and Friday. I'd be about eight years old, my brother would be four.

Catherine and Malcolm McManahan

(Catherine Pickard née McManahan)

When you went in, it was like a foyer, a newspaper stall under the roof, with the newspapers and magazines all laid out. You could buy them without having to go in the shop. The comics were on a rack. Mr Holderness, the manager, he'd given permission that me and my brother could read these comics, like Beano, Bunty, June, School Friend and Judy, and 'Look and Learn', a nature one. Bunty was good because you had the girl on the back and you could cut out the clothes and hook them onto the little figure. We were only allowed to read the comics then we had to put them back after my Mum had done her stint.

There were quite a lot of ladies worked there. Through the newspaper section were the

228

books. You went to the back of the store and it was toys. There was a little office where the cashier was. Upstairs they sold cards and downstairs was records.

W H Smith's record department, 1980s (Dawn Allerston)

We had to climb right up to the ladies' changing room. Then the ladies used to come, they wore 1960s clothes, I remember the mini skirts. There was an older lady, she used perfume. When she had a little bit left in her perfume bottle, she'd give it to me.

At Christmas Mr Holderness would let me and my brother choose a book. He gave me the 'Complete Works of the Brontës'. But I was only little and I noticed there was '101 Animal Stories', so I asked if I could have that instead. I regretted it years after because I was a Brontë fan.

We used to get this album full of cards, they were there for a business to send as a Christmas card. When they were finished with, Mr Holderness would give them to us. There were some beautiful cards in there.

I suppose quite a lot of childhood memories are centred on W H Smith's. We went there for a few years. It was nice because they were kind to us, letting us borrow the comics. We had to sit there for two hours. It kept us occupied.

Catherine's brother, Malcolm McManahan, also remembers,

We used to get, every Christmas, Blue Peter and Bimbo annuals. I remember buying the first edition of 'Look In' magazine.

In the basement there was a man who crushed all the cardboard with a machine,

a huge metal contraption which was used to press down large cardboard boxes, operated by a kind gentleman by the name of Mr King. I used to have this horrible fear of falling into it and getting crushed. I don't know if they did recycling back then.

Quite a lot of people worked in the basement, Mr Graham oversaw it all. He was nice as well. He gave me a big brown car, it was battery operated. I don't know whether I got it as a gift or because it was a bit faulty. I remember him giving me a Simon Snorkel fire engine. Obviously they were meant to be for sale but I think that had been slightly damaged. I had a lot of hours playing with that toy.

In 1977 W H Smith's moved further up Coney Street into the old Grisdale's shop at 39–41. York Archaeological Trust carried out an excavation on the site, which was just outside the south corner of the Roman legionary fortress, an important position close to the banks of the Ouse where the ships docked to go to the east coast. The Trust uncovered grain warehouses from the first and second century. The earlier warehouse had suffered an infestation, with a huge number of grain beetles and arable weeds found.

Dr Richard Hall at the excavation in Coney Street, 1974

(York Archaeological Trust)

The new shop was far bigger than the previous one, and before long the building was extended again. It is now something of a rabbit warren, with five floors, and more than 20 rooms. Many of the rooms on the top floors are used for storage, with hundreds of signs and fittings kept there. From the book department, the original external brick wall of Grisdale's can be seen, at the point where the new extension begins, cleverly covered by a glass ceiling. The staff room is now a large room at the far end of the store, above the book department, with windows overlooking the river.

Staircase at W H Smith (Van Wilson)

Dawn Allerston has worked there since she was 16 and is the longest serving member of staff.

They advertised in the Evening Press and I went for an interview in August 1978. Then I got a letter saying that I'd got a job

*in the book department. I was really pleased about that. My
normal working hours were 8.30 to 5.30 and my wage for
a 40-hour week was £26 exactly which in those days was
a fortune.*

*The shop was very much in departments. There was a store
manager and deputy, and a manager and deputy for each department – books, records, stationery, news, office and stockroom.
Toys came under stationery at the time. This store had a travel
agency as well. It lasted a few years then they sold it to Lunn
Poly. The W H Smith's logo [a cube], was on everything. When
we had a canteen, the plates, the saucers all had that logo round
the edge. Everything was branded.*

*I started on books. We didn't do work experience, your work
experience was your first day. I was terrified but the department
manager, Mrs Debenham, took me under her wing, taught me
everything. Her standards were so high, and she trained me and
I had her standards. And I still do. On a Monday when I first
started, every book was taken off the shelves and dusted, and
all the shelves were dusted.*

*I was lucky, I always stayed on books. Each store had a book
buyer, whereas now everything is centrally bought and sent
into the stores, it wasn't when I started. Mrs Debenham was
the book buyer and she trained me. So it was me the book reps
came to see, I decided what was going on the shelves and what
quantities. That was when I was in my early 20s. Then it got
streamlined and they decided that Smith's needed a more corpo-
rate image. So the book buying was taken into head office. I'm
still the local book buyer. I still use my skills. I'm passionate
about local books because I have a direct influence. It's getting
the balance right between what visitors want and what York
residents want.*

*The ground floor at the back was records, then stationery then
news at the front. Where the tills and cards are, that was a
separate shop, the Singer Sewing shop when I started. Then
upstairs we had books, toys and games. The Singer shop became
Salisbury's handbags and when they closed we got that shop
and it was knocked through to make one bigger shop. We had
records and cassettes. And then as cassettes fell out of favour
and records, it was CDs and videos. We had a big pen counter,
and we sold typewriters, calculators and cameras.*

Many bookshops in York have disappeared, such as Pickering's,
Godfrey's, Penguin Bookshop, Claude Gill, Dillons and Borders,
though we still have Smith's, Waterstones, Little Apple and the
Barbican, as well as some good second hand bookshops.

*A lot of the independents have gone, and even though they were
competitors, it's a pity they've gone, for the book lover. A lot of
Borders' customers came here. We had a bigger book range than
they realised, and certainly things like science fiction, fantasy
and graphic novels, those sales took off. And literary fiction as
well, we started selling a lot more. Some people don't realise
there's a book department upstairs. More than one customer
has said it's like the Tardis in here. At the front the shop looks
narrow but it does expand out and goes a long way back.
Smith's more than doubled the size of the store.*

*We have a café, Costa Coffee. That's a concession. When I first
came there was a canteen and a fully staffed kitchen. Morning
break they did toast, or in winter they did bacon sandwiches.
Lunchtime they'd make up sandwiches or a cooked meal every
day. The best day was a Friday because they did a Sunday
lunch, so one week chicken, then pork, then beef, and Yorkshire puddings, roast potatoes. And it was about 65p for this
full meal. They baked every day so on your afternoon break it*

W H Smith's book department staff, 1970s. Dawn Allerston on far left, Mrs Isa Debenham
with white cap at front. (Dawn Allerston)

was always cakes. It's a wonder we got any work done. That
closed in 1996. It was a financial decision but it was sad when
it closed. They used to do a full Christmas dinner every year.
Any profit went to pay for days out. At the time we didn't open
Sundays, or bank holidays and there was no late night shop-
ping. We used to hire a coach and go to TV studios at Granada
or we went to Beamish one year.

It's a totally different environment now. When I came there were
no computers so all stock was counted by hand. Now with the
computers we just swipe the item, it's logged it's been sold and
it's reordered. We don't need as many staff. One of the tills we
had, if there was a power cut, we used to fold down the side and
it could be hand cranked so we've gone from, in an emergency,
hand cranking a till to fully automated. [The shop also has self-
service machines.]

The book department when I started, there was six full-time and three part-time members of staff. Then we had people just on the tills. Now upstairs during the week there's two full-time and a part-time member of staff and our supervisor. We have a very small section of CDs and DVDs downstairs. We sell mainly bestsellers.

The first Christmas that we opened late, the first late night shopping, we all dressed up. One year they got several train carriages and kitted them out as a bookshop and it went from station to station. It stopped in a siding and then authors joined the train and did signing sessions. And the staff from the local store manned the shop. It was the early 80s. World Book Day, we dress up for that. One year we took part in the Lord Mayor's parade, promoting our travel agency. 'We're far from stationery when it comes to travel'.

Over the last few years, the Harry Potter books have been the best-sellers.

Harry Potter Day at W H Smith, 1990s: left to right, ?, Fiona Gregg, Ben Potter, Dawn Allerston (Dawn Allerston)

For the new J K Rowlings, Harry Potter, we all dressed up. They provided the plain black cloaks and the hats and I decorated them [with owls and stars].

In 2012 the bestseller was 'Fifty Shades of Grey'.

That took us all by surprise. We were selling hundreds every week, it was amazing. It has continued to a degree, there's a lot more authors writing in that genre.

The biggest signing session we had was Terry Pratchett. That was unbelievable. Ian Botham came, that was extremely popular, we had them queuing down the store, round the fixtures. And when Noel Edmonds came, when Swap Shop [Saturday morning children's TV programme] *was on, we had to have the police controlling the crowds. We provided refreshments. It used to be my job to go to Marks and Spencer's and buy the food and wine.*

My first uniform was like an overall in blue with green on cuffs and pockets. Then we went into a brown pinafore and blouse. Then a grey pinafore which made us look like prison warders. Then a beige skirt, a blouse and navy jacket. We now have the Kobo, and the Smiths' that have a Kobo store within them, the staff wear the Kobo branded uniforms. Kindle is American, Kobo is Canadian. You can store 1000 books on there. It's surprised me how they've taken off. But our book sales have held their own. They still sell exceptionally well. I can tell people about Kobo but my love is the traditional book and I'll be fighting their corner till the day I retire.

The store manager, Chris Price, has his office in a lovely room facing Coney Street which retains the panelling and fireplaces from the time of Grisdale's.

Dawn Allerston and Chris Price at W H Smith
(Christine Kyriacou)

The old part of the building is beautiful. The rooms at the very very top, I assume they were the servants quarters originally, they used to say they were very hot in summer and freezing cold in winter.

I've been very lucky. My absolute passion is books. It's a good company to work for. A lot of people have been customers as long as I've been here. I get comments like, 'Are you still here?', which is nice. There will always be awkward customers but they're far outweighed by the nice customer. I once had a customer return a get well card to me and ask for a refund because the person had died. Then a lady returned a CD because the needle on her record player kept slipping off it!

Retail has changed so much, it's very much about profit, and customers are very very important. You felt like you were part of a family, but then the retail market started to change and Smith's started to lose some of its business, so it had to think very businesslike and the changes came in. We were getting more competitors. We have to make a profit in order to survive.

— Chapter 12 —
CONEY STREET BUSINESSES

Coney Street has been the scene over the years of almost every kind of business. As well as shops, there have long been solicitor's and account-ants' offices, servants' registries, car showrooms, music studios, piano warehouse and banks. The National Westminster Bank on the corner of New Street, built by Brierley in 1907, is now Starbuck's, and the bank has moved to the corner of Market Street and Spurriergate. The Yorkshire Bank of 1922, designed by Chorley, Gibbon and Elcock, is still in its original building.

BURGIN'S

Burgin's perfumery, opposite the Mansion House, which began as a chemist in 1880, is the oldest shop in Coney Street. It has only had four proprietors, Mark Burgin who set up the business, Jeremy Wright, who took over in 1934, and changed it into a perfumery, 'selling sex and snobbery to the people of York', June Yeo, who ran the business from 1997 to 2011, and the present owner Hanus Wolf.

The shop offers more than 1200 fragrances and states that, 'Knowledge-able staff dispense fragrance just like the pharmacists of yesteryear'. The range of perfumes includes classic fragrances

Two Efficient Remedies

Influenza and Cold Mixture.

Nothing else acts so quickly as this—and nothing is so certain to arrest the development of severe chill. It prevents severe prostration and subsequent weakness. **1/6 a Bottle**

Bismuth Mixture.

Affords immediate relief in case of Dyspepsia accompanied with pain after eating, is specially recommended for stomachic affections.
1/6 & 2/6 per Bottle. Makes a good digestion

OBTAINABLE FROM

Mark F. Burgin
(Proprietor J. A. WRIGHT, M.P.S.)

MANSION HOUSE
PHARMACY

54, CONEY STREET
YORK.

'Phone 3137.
Telegrams: BURGIN, CHEMIST. YORK

10

Burgin's advert

239

from Chanel and Elizabeth Arden; the exotic Soir de Paris made by Bourjois in 1928, floral and old fashioned, Guerlain's Mitsouko of 1919, a gold medal winner, right up the present day perfumes launched by such celebrities as Avril Lavigne, Beyoncé and David Beckham.

Whenever you use your lipstick and powder puff, you need your perfume also

Coty

introduce the

"PURSER"

a new and beautiful perfume container
FOR THE HANDBAG
Just the thing that women have been wanting for years. Beautifully designed and solidly constructed, this gold-tone case is non-breakable and non-spillable. The caps are made in 4 different colours to match the fashionable handbag shades.

Filled with
L'Aimant, L'Origan, Paris, Chypre, Le Nouveau Gardenia or Muguet   3/9

OBTAINABLE FROM

MARK F. BURGIN
(Proprietor: J. A. WRIGHT, M.P.S.)

MANSION HOUSE PHARMACY,
54, Coney Street, York.

Burgin's advert

Glyn Meek and Theresa Rayner at Burgin's, 2013 (Christine Kyriacou)

King George VI and Queen Elizabeth outside Burgin's, 1940s

CHAPMAN AND WILSON

Anne Sains's father worked at Lipton's grocer's, near

Chapman and Wilson at number 36 in 1900. They were stationers. I have a friend in a care home who worked there. She was 15 when she went there [in 1942], and she used to operate this great big roller printer, printing private addresses onto note-paper. It was quite a hard job.

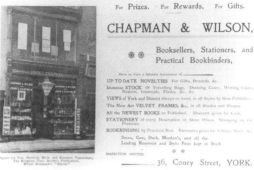

For Prizes. For Rewards. For Gifts.

CHAPMAN & WILSON,

Booksellers, Stationers, and Practical Bookbinders,

Here on View a Splendid Assortment of—

UP-TO-DATE NOVELTIES For Gifts, Rewards, &c.
Immense STOCK Of Travelling Bags, Dressing Cases, Writing Cases, Baskets, Inkstands, Flasks, &c., &c.
VIEWS of York and District always on hand, in all Styles by Best Publishers.
The New Art VELVET FRAMES, &c., in all Shades and Shapes.
All the NEWEST BOOKS as Published. Discount given for Cash.
STATIONERY of every Description at Store Prices. Stamping on the Premises.
BOOKBINDING by Practical Men. Estimates given for Library Work, &c.
Swan, Caw, Duck, Mordan's, and all the Leading Reservoir and Stylo Pens kept in Stock.

INSPECTION INVITED.

_____36, Coney Street, YORK.

Chapman and Wilson advert

THOMAS COOK TRAVEL AGENT

Thomas Cook, Britain's oldest travel agency, which began nationally in 1841, was based at 38 Coney Street. A government information bureau opened on the premises during the First World War in August 1918.

There were big alterations to the front and interior in 1938 and plans for a new shop front in 1961. The business moved to Nessgate in April 1981.

Chapman and Wilson shop

(York Oral History Society)

241

THOMAS COOKE

Thomas Cooke, optician, ran his business at 12 Coney Street in 1844. He went on to manufacture refracting telescopes, optical instruments, and turret clocks. He built the factory in Bishophill and moved there in 1855. In 1922 the company became Cooke, Troughton and Simms. This was very successful, eventually moving to Haxby Road and being taken over by Vicker's. The observatory in the Museum Gardens and at Bootham School still use Cooke's telescopes.

HORSLEY GUN MANUFACTURERS

Thomas Horsley, the gun manufacturer, was founded in 1830 originally in Stonegate, then moved to 10 Coney Street, with a branch in Blossom Street, and was later at 48 Coney Street. He moved to part of the George Inn premises in April 1856 and had a workshop behind the shop. In February 1862 the first British snap action patent was granted to him. In 1885 the company was advertising as a 'gun and rifle manufacturer', but also sold outdoor sporting equipment and ran a shooting range. A gentleman wrote to The Field magazine that 'All the gentlemen in Yorkshire shoot with Horsley guns'.

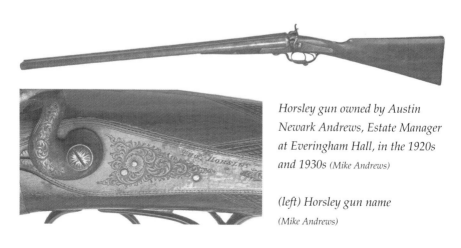

Horsley gun owned by Austin Newark Andrews, Estate Manager at Everingham Hall, in the 1920s and 1930s (Mike Andrews)

(left) Horsley gun name (Mike Andrews)

The shop was advertised for sale in 1914 and moved to Micklegate just before the Second World War. An intriguing story from 'Shooting Times' in 2008, by Robin Marshall-Ball, tells how a rare Horsley gun from a small Texas town, found its way back to England.

It was a double 4 made by Thomas Horsley of York. The gun still had the original leather case and the top tray contained 24 brass cases head-stamped T. Horsley. The gun itself had Horsley's patent pull-back top-lever opening as well as a bar-in-the-wood action, which was elegant, functional and extremely rare in a gun of this size. Horsley's records showed that the gun was made for a Captain Ingham in 1870, and it was probably one of only three bar-in-the-wood double 4-bores made by Horsley.

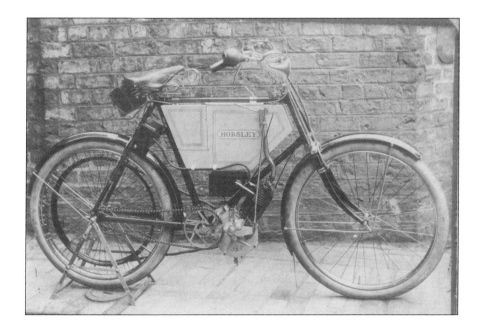

Horsley motorised bicycle (York Oral History Society)

So, on a windswept and cold dawn during next wildfowling season, Captain Ingham, looking down from that great salt-marsh in the sky, will hear the clamour of geese and the mighty boom of a 4-bore. He'll smile to himself and exclaim, 'I know that voice!'

Moyra Johnson, who was born in 1915 and was related to the family, recalls,

The Horsleys were very inventive, they developed their own car. I went to London in it, I was about 12. We went to the Motor Show and Uncle Tom drove. The Horsleys had a sister who lived in Shepherd's Bush, Aunty Florrie, and it was with her that we stayed. You can imagine what it must have been like in those days, an open car. Sometimes you had to go backwards, I remember Daddy saying that he'd been up Sutton Bank backwards.

Horsley gun manufacturers (Moyra Johnson)

I had some cousins ten years older than me at Scarborough, called Sonny and Pansy. They told me that when they used to come through to see Grandad and Grandma at 20 Coney Street, Mrs Horsley, the grandmother, [she was French] *a Villerette, always wore black, and the children had to curtsey. I think they would have come over at the French revolution, I've got silver spoons with RAV on – R.A. Villerette.*

Roland Newey, father of Geoffrey Newey, of the well known York clockmaker's firm,

worked on the bench at Horsley's. In those days the workmen wore top hats. The shop front went into the Castle Museum [when it eventually closed].

Moyra did not go into the family business,

I would have loved to have done, but I was a woman. I knew that I couldn't take over. My cousin Tony was a good ten years younger than me, he wasn't interested in guns. His son Nick, that would have been a different story, he loves the guns and he's an engineer.

INGLIS JEWELLERS

In the 19th century, there were a number of jewellers and clockmakers in the city centre. The 1880 York street directory includes John Arundel, a manufacturing jeweller's and silversmith's at 22 Coney Street, Miss Elizabeth Epworth who ran a jeweller's shop at 14 Spurriergate and Robert Heselgrave, a jeweller and clockmaker at 12 Coney Street. Darling and Wood at 42 Coney Street, and George Heselwood at 51 Coney Street were clockmakers.

Probably the most famous was James Inglis, who became a watch-maker, jeweller and engraver in 1885, having trained at Goldsmith's in London, and moving to Coney Street in about 1900. He became Sheriff in 1911 and Lord Mayor in 1922.

His advertisement stated,

His stock of silver and electro-plate ranks are second to none in York for exquisite design, tasteful selection and high-class workmanship, drawn from the best houses in Sheffield and London. Mr Inglis holds a catalogue of over 5000 designs. Of watches, he holds one of the largest stocks in the city and claims that his prices are as low as any firm in York.

Inglis advert (Kelly's directory)

He makes a speciality of medals, club badges, sport prizes and presentation goods. There are workshops and showrooms for clocks and bronzes, and where a wedding ring may be fitted without fear of interruption. Instead of waiting for the corporation to supply electricity, Mr Inglis put down a small installation to light his premises, and his shop fittings are quite up to date.

In 1914, the shop was advertising items useful for the war,

> *a large range of field glasses including Dolland, Zeiss and all principal makers, special stock of wristwatches and luminous watches suitable for active service. During the absence of Mr A Inglis on military service, the optical and cutlery department will be attended to personally by Mr J B Inglis.*

The York Civic and Gala week brochure in June 1934 advertised,

> *J B Inglis, high class jewellers. The finest selection of gem rings in the city, prices from 50s to £50. All carry a three year guarantee. Famous for half a century for purity, colour and reflective quality.*

Mr James Barker worked at Inglis when it moved out of Coney Street, eventually becoming managing director. He explains,

> *Inglis were at 4 Coney Street. His services were repairing and engraving and work was done in Castlegate. They also crown plated and nickel plated, gilded, enamelled and lacquered. They did everything for the jewellery trade. He also, at one point, made his own silver polish.*

> *He then moved to the other end of Coney Street where Debenham's used to be. They were there for a number of years. J B Inglis had three sons, one emigrated to Canada, Rob Inglis looked after the jewellery side and Alec Inglis looked after the optician's. Rob was trained in house by his father. During the Second World War the jewellery side virtually closed down because of the shortage of goods. They opened up in Stonegate straight after the war.*

> *We employed 23 staff at one point. I was sales person initially when I started and I eventually made my way up to managing*

J. B. INGLIS & SONS,

Sole District Agents for the
"WYLER" UNBREAKABLE WATCH.

The watch which was dropped from Eiffel Tower (975 ft.) and picked up intact and going perfectly.

The Ideal Watch for Motorists, Airmen, Athletes, Golfers, and all Sportsmen.

PRICES FROM
£3 3s. 0d.

There are many unbreakable watches on the market but only one which will stand the test.

IT MUST BE THE
"WYLER."

The watch which has been dropped from an aeroplane from a height of 1,400 ft. and picked up in perfect going order.

"**York House," Coney Street, YORK.**

Inglis advert

director and eventually I owned the business. David Inglis retired and I carried on for about 10 or 11 years then I sold it to Berry's of Leeds. They kept the name of Inglis for another 20 years.

It changed dramatically from the early days. We eventually came onto battery operated watches as opposed to winding watches. We used to sell silver plated and solid silver cutlery, then we finished up selling nearly all stainless steel because people didn't want to be bothered cleaning it.

Adrian Gell also worked for J B Inglis in Stonegate. His full story is told in 'Stonegate Voices'. But his apprenticeship was in Coney Street.

I started at Grant's next door to Woolworth's and I had seven years of quite hard work. My first week's wage was nine shillings, which after seven years became 30 shillings at the age of 21. So it was quite hard financially. But they were very good teachers, it was a family concern. The man who taught on the repair side was extremely good. When he came to my 21st party, he said I could call him Mr Hatch, up to then it was always Sir. I was never allowed to call him Gordon. I'd made it, in other words I'd pleased him.

When I first went to the interview. I walked into the room and I don't know how I stood it, just one mass of clocks ticking. The noise was out of this world. It was a cacophony. The walls were full of clocks and watches hung on hooks. You would never have believed you could talk amongst that noise, but after that you never heard it. It just accepts it, the brain.

LEOPARD ARCADE

The Leopard Arcade is remembered now mainly because it was totally destroyed in the 1942 Baedeker raid on York. It stood on the site of the Leopard Inn which had been demolished in 1924. With a balcony all the way round and shops above and below, it was a favourite area. Before the war, the arcade housed costumiers, dyers, milliners, opticians and the Northern Motor Utilities showroom. Joan Sadler recalls,

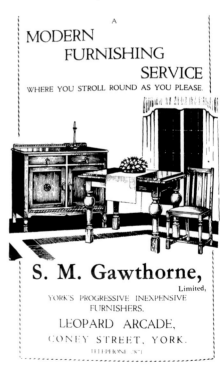

A
MODERN
FURNISHING
SERVICE
WHERE YOU STROLL ROUND AS YOU PLEASE.

I've always loved shops with being brought up in the heart of the city. The Leopard Arcade was lovely. Saxone shoe shop I remember well. That was at the bottom. As you went into the arcade there was a balcony and a hairdresser, Pierre, he had a business there.

Between 3am and 6am on the morning of 29 April 1942, the official report stated that

S. M. Gawthorne,
Limited,
YORK'S PROGRESSIVE INEXPENSIVE FURNISHERS.

LEOPARD ARCADE,
CONEY STREET, YORK.
TELEPHONE 281

Gawthorne, Leopard Arcade advert

there were 'fires in Coney street, with the danger of masonry from the Leopard Arcade falling on three firemen who were directing the hose on St Martin's Church. The national fire servicemen were fighting the fire in New Street at the Tower cinema. By morning the cinema had been saved but the Arcade was gone'. A few days later a lady who had taken shoes in to be repaired in the arcade, returning to collect them, found that not only were there no shoes, but there was no shoe shop left.

Maison Lee advert, 1963 (Kelly's directory)

MAISON LEE

Maison Lee was known for many years as the best hair salon in York, only challenged for the title by Swallow and Barry. Mr Jerome, Mr Lee's manager, was an American who brought modern ideas to the place. In 1963 he offered 'a movement wave which will give body and line to hair from 35s'. (A styled shampoo and set cost 7/6d). He began to cater for different age groups, such as teenagers and pre-teens.

STEAD AND SIMPSON

Stead and Simpson began in Leeds as curriers and leather dealers in 1834, later moving into shoe manufacture and moving its base to Leicester. The business expanded throughout the 20th century and in 2008 was bought by Shoe Zone. But stores began to close within a few years.

SHOES

For Spring & Summer

THOSE who are desirous of purchasing Footwear of any description are invited to visit our new and finely-equipped Branch at

14, CONEY STREET,

where they will have the opportunity of inspecting Boots and Shoes for every purpose, and where they may be certain of receiving the utmost courtesy and most painstaking attention in the matter of fitting.

Every purchase can be relied upon for absolute soundness, for smartness of style, for weather-resisting properties and for durability, and the extent of our trading operations all over the Country enable us to sell at prices which represent the maximum of value for the money spent.

The opening of this new Branch has been rendered necessary by the great extension of our business in York, and it is in no way intended to take the place of our already existing depot at 5, HIGH OUSEGATE.

STEAD & SIMPSON,
Limited.

Stead and Simpson advert, 1910

Stead and Simpson opened a store at High Ousegate and found business was very good, so in 1910 they opened a second branch at 14 Coney Street, one of several shoe shops in the street. The shop had departments for men, women and children.

Susan Natt left school in 1969 and went to work there.

You went in and on the right hand side there was the most enormous rocking horse, it was absolutely beautiful.

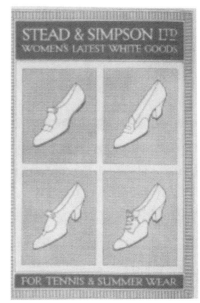

Stead and Simpson advert, 1920s

Stead and Simpson on left, 1950s (Ian Collinson)

Even the adults sometimes went on it, I got on myself a couple of times, but it was really for children.

Just beyond that there was a staircase down into the basement. When you got down the stairs, there was a large office which was the cashier's desk. There was these four tubes, it was called a Lamson. And they'd put the money from the various levels into tubes and twist them, and then we used to press a button and air would take them down to the cash desk. [An example of this can be found on youtube.com.] *At one point I became cashier so I was in the little office most of the time taking the cash and finishing off the books at night.*

Down at the bottom, on the right hand side, was the ladies' department. Beyond that were big double doors which led out into a garden. This garden would flood, and the rats would come up, so we'd have to keep the door shut even in summer. It used to leave all the debris, it was horrible. An external door led into the flat above. That's what we used for storage. The main lounge was at the front, the bedrooms were enormous. I remember this big bathroom, and an enormous old-fashioned bath.

I used to come to work on the bike. Behind the shop in High Ousegate, there's a yard with a bike shed and an alleyway up to it with a locked door. The manager had the key. I used to park my bike in there. One day I'd gone at half past five and I heard this noise. When I looked he'd locked the door with me inside the yard. So I was frantic. I was only 15. It was starting to get dark and I started to shout through the letter box. And this little boy came. Luckily he found a policeman and the policeman said, "Don't panic love, I know there's a back way". He came round and suddenly appeared at the wall, this bobby's helmet. He said, "Do you think you can climb up?" And sure enough there was an alleyway that went back out into Peter Lane. Once I got to

Stead and Simpson. L to R: Sheila Henderson, Sheena Burke, Susan Watson now Natt, unknown, Jane Trapps. c. 1969. (Susan Natt)

the other side I could just drop down. I got on the bus with dirty hands and dirty face and I wasn't very happy with the manager the next day. He just brushed it off. Nobody would have known I was there if this little boy hadn't gone to get a policeman. He never came back so I never got to thank him.

My mother in law used to work at Leak and Thorp [next door]. When I was courting my husband, she'd come into Stead and Simpson's and bring cream cakes. And I used to share them with my colleagues.

Decimalisation came in [in 1971] and I remember the manager taking us to one side and testing us. I got it straight off but I had a head for figures which is why I ended up cashier. And I also went as a relief manageress a couple of times to different branches in Leeds and Malton.

We prided ourselves on seating people down, measuring feet and spending time with people. You could spend hours with one customer, you could get 20, 30 pairs of shoes out on the floor around us. The sizes went from 3s mainly to 7s. We had a couple of customers that took size 8s, but they didn't have much choice them days. These days the youngsters are size 8, 9 and 10s. If somebody came into Stead and Simpson's they wanted to buy a pair of shoes. They knew they would get the service.

We used to dye white satin shoes for weddings. Once we'd sold them, we'd match them with the colour that they wanted, blues, pinks, even red. It was so simple. We sold anything shoe orientated, polish, laces, shoe horns, boot shapers.

And when we went to the new shop it was self service and we didn't like it, and our customers didn't like it. Once we changed shops, there was no room for the rocking horse. It wasn't a very nice shop. It was all on one level. There was a big cellar down below along with our staff room.

We used to get inmates from Askham Richard prison coming in. They were always with a guard in uniform. They were allowed £5 and they had to buy two or three pairs of shoes.

We used to get staff discount. I remember some thigh boots coming in and they were £5 and they were leather. I put a pair aside for myself and I saved up for them. When you were only getting a couple of pounds a week, it's a lot of money. They were tucked away in a little cupboard with my name on. When I left it was about £4-15s a week. It was a traditional shop. It's all self-service now. People rush, they don't have time.

Today the face of Coney Street has changed dramatically from its earlier self. Boots, W H Smith's (though both have moved to different premises in the street) and Burgin's still exist, but most of the elegant traditional shops, the family businesses which took pride in personal service and a relationship with customers, have gone.

Coney Street in 2013 from St Martin's Church roof (Mike Race)

Our ancestors would be astonished if they could see our high streets today. In Coney Street there are still dress and accessory stores, but also a Chinese herbal clinic, two nightclubs, American-owned coffee shops, and amplified buskers in shop doorways. Perhaps the biggest change is that of the mobile phone stores, of which there are currently eight in Coney Street!

Fortunately we are still able to access memories, documents and newspapers, as well as wonderful photographs, to build up a picture of what the street was like in the past.

BIBLIOGRAPHY

Cooper, T. F. *The Old Inns and Inn Signs of York*. DeLittle & Sons, The City Press. 1897

Knight, C. B. *A History of the City of York*. Herald Printing Works. 1944.

Murray, Hugh. *Directory of York Pubs*. Voyager Publications. 2004.

Murray, Hugh. *Pedigrees of York Families*.

Royal Commission on Historical Monuments. *York. Vol. V. The Central Area*. Royal Commission on Historical Monuments. 1981

Stacpool, Alberic. *The Noble City of York*. Cerialis Press. 1972

Tillott, P.M. ed. *A History of Yorkshire: The City of York*. Oxford University Press. 1961

York Civic Week Committee. *York Civic and Gala Week June 1934*. Herald Printing Works 1934

Archive of Anderson the Tailor (in York Explore Local History and Archives)

Kinematograph Weekly 1937

York and County Times Spring and Summer 1963

York City Council Minute Books

York City Screen Programme January 2000

York Illustrated 1911

York Shopping Week 1910 Brochure

York Street Directories – Kelly's and White's

Yorkshire Evening Press (now The Press)

Yorkshire Evening Press. Supplement to mark the end of 255 years of printing in Coney Street. July 1989

Yorkshire Gazette and Herald

Yorkshire Herald

Yorkshire Illustrated April 1953

www.boots.com.

www.thespurriergatecentre.com

www.whsmith.com

PUBLICATIONS BY THE SAME AUTHOR

The History of a Community : Fulford Road District of York. University College of Ripon and York St John, 1984. (Reprinted 1985)

Alexina : A Woman in Wartime York. Voyager Publications, 1995

Rich in all but Money: Life in Hungate 1900–1938. York Archaeological Trust, 1996. (Reprinted 1997. Revised edition 2007)

Beyond the Postern Gate: A History of Fishergate and Fulford Road. York Archaeological Trust, 1996

Humour, Heartache and Hope : Life in Walmgate. York Archaeological Trust, 1996

York Voices. Tempus Publishing, 1999

Number 26 : The History of 26 St Saviourgate. Voyager Publications,1999

Voices of St Paul's: An Oral History of St Paul's Church. (Edited) William Sessions, 2001

Rhythm and Romance: An Oral History of Popular Music in York. Volume 1: The Dance Band Years. York Oral History Society, 2002

Something in the Air: An Oral History of Popular Music in York. Volume 2: The Beat Goes On. York Oral History Society, 2002

Rhythm and Romance: CD of The York Dance Band Era. York Oral History Society, 2003

The Walmgate Story. Voyager Publications, 2006. (Reprinted 2009 and 2011)

Something in the Air: CD of York Music in 1960s. York Oral History Society, 2006

Rations, Raids and Romance: York in the Second World War. York Archaeological Trust, 2008 (Reprinted 2009)

Stonegate Voices. York Archaeological Trust, 2009.

The Story of Terry's. York Oral History Society, 2009

The Best Years of Our Lives : Secondary Education in York 1900–1985. York Archaeological Trust, 2010

The Changing Face of Clifton. York Archaeological Trust, 2011 (Reprinted 2012)

It's How You Play the Game: Olympic Sports in York. York Archaeological Trust, 2012